Meanings into Words
Intermediate

Student's Book

Meanings into Words
Intermediate

An integrated course for students of English

Student's Book

Adrian Doff, Christopher Jones and Keith Mitchell

Cambridge University Press

Cambridge
London   New York   New Rochelle
Melbourne   Sydney

Published by the Press Syndicate of the University of Cambridge
The Pitt Building, Trumpington Street, Cambridge CB2 1RP
32 East 57th Street, New York, NY 10022, USA
10 Stamford Road, Oakleigh, Melbourne 3166, Australia

© Cambridge University Press 1983

First published 1983
Eighth printing 1986

Printed in Great Britain
at the University Press, Cambridge

ISBN 0 521 28283 7 Student's Book
ISBN 0 521 28286 1 Teacher's Book
ISBN 0 521 28284 5 Workbook
ISBN 0 521 28285 3 Test Book
ISBN 0 521 23887 0 Cassette (Student's Book)
ISBN 0 521 23888 9 Cassette (Drills)

KY

Contents

Introduction

This is the first of the two *Meanings into Words* Student's Books. It contains 24 units, each of which is based on a major functional or notional area of English. Each unit includes:
- Presentation material which introduces key language items.
- Intensive controlled practice.
- Freer communicative practice and writing activities.
- Listening and reading passages.
- A Language Summary which lists the main points covered in the unit.

After every two units (starting at Unit 4) there is an Activities page. These activities give an opportunity to combine and extend the language learnt in earlier units.

Meanings into Words Intermediate Student's Book is accompanied by:
- A *Workbook* which contains extra written practice of the language taught in each unit.
- A *Test Book* which contains six Progress Tests and a Final Achievement Test.
- *Drills* (on cassette) which give intensive manipulation practice of key structures introduced in the unit, for use in the language laboratory.
- A *Teacher's Book* which includes a general description of the course as well as detailed teaching notes on each unit.
- A *Cassette* of all recorded material in the Student's Book.

Acknowledgements

The authors and publishers would like to express their thanks and appreciation to the following institutions for their invaluable assistance in testing the course material and helping the authors to make many necessary improvements: The Bell College, Saffron Walden; The Bell School, Cambridge; The Bell School, Norwich; NATO, Brussels, Belgium; The Newnham Language Centre, Cambridge; The Studio School of English, Cambridge; The University of Lyon, France. Parts of the material have also been tested by the authors at the British Council, Beirut and Stevenson College, Edinburgh.

The authors would like to give special thanks to David Jolly and David Scarbrough, whose wide-ranging ideas about communicative language learning have contributed much to the development of this course. They would also like to thank the following people for their contributions to the recorded material: Carolyn Becket, Gregor Graham, Josephine Jones, Sheena McDonald, Patrick Rayner and Doreen Taylor.

The authors and publishers are grateful to the following for permission to reproduce photographs, illustrations and texts: The British Tourist Authority (photographs on pp. 6, 13, 41, 70); British Airports Authority (photograph on p. 17); Ronelle's Discotheque, Cambridge (photograph on p. 17); *The Sunday Times* (article on p. 20); Gerald Duckworth & Co. Ltd (illustration on pp. 24 and 181 from *Inventions* by Heath Robinson); *Private Eye* (passage and illustration on p. 49); Richard and Sally Greenhill (photographs on p. 63 – nurse and policeman, 73, 74, 79, 93 – bottom left and top right, 101, 140 – top left, bottom left and top right, 159 – left and right); David Lewis (miner on p. 63); Dona Haycraft (teacher on p. 63); Chefaro Proprietaries Ltd (Bergasol advert on p. 64); Bryan and Cherry Alexander (photographs on p. 67); The Mansell Collection Ltd (illustrations on p. 68); Barnaby's Picture Library (photographs on pp. 93 – top middle, 140 – bottom right and middle left, 174); Sylvester Jacobs (photograph on p. 93 – top left); Space Frontiers Ltd (photograph on p. 95); Hodder and Stoughton Educational (article on p. 126); *Cambridge Evening News* (photograph on p. 140 – middle right); Hamlyn Paperbacks (article on p. 141); *The Guardian* (article and photograph on pp. 155 and 156); John Walmsley (photograph on p. 159 – middle); John Topham Picture Library (photographs on pp. 169 and 170); The Scottish Health Education Group (poster on p. 172); The Samaritans (advert on p. 173); Shelter National Campaign for the Homeless (advert on p. 173); Spokes and Jerry Neville (cartoon on p. 177); Mercedes-Benz, Levi Strauss & Co., London Transport and Diner's Club (p. 115).

The photographs on pp. 2, 3, 14, 17 – office, hotel, theatre and hospital, 59, 63 – lorry driver, 93 – bottom right, were taken by Nigel Luckhurst. The illustrations on pp. 1, 2, 22, 23, 25, 26, 27, 59, 60, 113, 114, 123, 139, 143, 144, 160 and 165 were drawn by **Chris Evans**; on pp. 4, 11, 16, 19, 33, 71, 98 and 159 by **John Walsh**; on pp. 9, 31, 44, 51, 53, 76, 87, 91, 106, 108, 121, 130, 137, 145, 146, 166 and 179 by **Dave Parkins**; on pp. 38 and 39 by **Brian Warwick**; on p. 47 by **William Le Fever**; on pp. 116, 118, 125 and 135 by **Reg Piggott**.

Book designed by Peter Ducker MSTD

Unit 1　Places

1.1　ROOMS AND FURNITURE

Presentation

You will hear a phone conversation between a landlady and a student who is looking for a room.

1　Mark the window of Stephen's room on the picture.

2　Which is Stephen's room?

3 What is the name of the landlady's street?

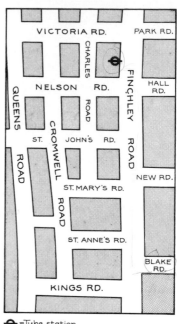

4 According to the landlady, where are the following?
   a) the room
   b) the divan bed
   c) the desk
   d) the lamp
   e) the bathroom
   f) the toilet
   g) the kitchenette
   h) the electric kettle

☊ =Tube station

Practice

Work in pairs.
Student A: You are Stephen. Ask the landlady questions about the room.
Student B: You are the landlady. Answer Stephen's questions.

1.2 WHERE THINGS ARE   Practice

Look at the room below. Say what there is in it and where each thing is, using words from the box.

by	in	below	between
beside	on	under	behind
next to	opposite	above	in front of
		over	

2

Now say where things are in the room you are in now.

1.3 YOUR OWN ROOM

Free practice

Work in pairs.
Student A: Tell your partner about your own room or flat. Describe it in as much detail as possible.
Student B: Take brief notes. Ask your partner further questions if necessary.

Writing

From your notes, write a description of your partner's room.

1.4 SERVICES

Presentation

At most hotels, they make your
bed and wash your clothes.
You can **have** your bed **made**.
You can **have** your clothes
washed.

1 What else can you have done
   at most hotels?
2 What can you have done at
   the Supercontinental?

At the Supercontinental we really take care of you

At most hotels they make your
bed, wash your clothes, clean your shoes,
and bring drinks to your room.

At the Supercontinental, we do
all that and more.

Your suit needs cleaning? Just
give it to our 2-hour dry-cleaning service.

You need to smarten up? Visit
our hairdressing salon and we'll wash
and cut your hair, trim your beard, and
manicure your fingernails - even your
toenails, if you like.

You have urgent business? We
have a staff of highly trained secret-
aries, who will type letters for you, and
send cables to any part of the world.

It's all part of the service - you
don't have to lift a finger!

Supercontinental
Tel: 537-45515/6

Practice

All the places below provide services. Write in their names.

Hairdresser's

What can you have done at each of these places?

1.5 ASKING ABOUT SERVICES   Practice

Example: Your hair's too long.
>   A: I want to have my hair cut. Do you know a good hairdresser's around
>   here?
>   B: I usually have mine cut at Toni's.
>   A: Toni's? Where's that exactly?
>   B: It's in Davies Street, opposite the cinema.

Have similar conversations, using the ideas below. Give true answers if you can.

1 Your sheets are dirty.
2 You're worried about your eyesight.
3 Your car needs servicing.
4 You've just finished a film in your camera.

5 You need a new suit.
6 The sole has come off your shoe.
7 You need some photocopies of a document.

1.6 AMENITIES

Presentation

What different kinds of places can you think of:
1 where you can stay for a few nights?
2 where you can find something to read?
3 where you can get some fresh air and exercise?
4 where you can take your children for a day out?
5 where you can follow your cultural interests?
6 where you can spend a night out?

Practice

Make sentences about each of the places you thought of. Give one important piece of information about each place, using **which** or **where**, as in the examples.

Example: Spending a night out
  There are night clubs, **which** stay open till 4 o'clock in the morning.
  There are pubs, **where** you can sit and have a glass of beer.
  There are . . .

1.7 TALKING ABOUT AMENITIES   Free practice

You will hear a conversation in which someone tells a visitor about different places to stay in his town.
1 What different places does he mention?
2 What information does he give about each one?

Place	Information

Now have similar conversations about your own town. Talk about:
1 different places to stay
2 different things to do on a sunny day

3 different things to do on a rainy day
4 different places to go in the evening

5

Reading

Along the coast 6

Torquay

Continuing our series on British seaside resorts, Kay Mellish visits the high spot of the 'English Riviera'.

Situated in the South West of England, between Exeter and Plymouth, Torquay is one of the most popular holiday resorts in Britain. It provides sophisticated entertainment, sports of
5 every kind and cultural facilities, all set in a position of outstanding natural beauty. Visitors can choose between luxury hotels by the sea, with private suites, swimming pools and saunas, and comfortable but less expensive guest
10 houses. There are camping sites, too, and hundreds of houses displaying 'B & B' signs.

As well as a number of secluded coves (which are ideal for beach barbecues away from the crowds), Torquay has large sandy beaches
15 where you can buy refreshments and hire deck chairs, boats and even beach huts. There are large areas of grassland overlooking the sea, and miles of winding cliff paths for walkers who just want to enjoy the scenery and what is often said
20 to be the healthiest air in the country. For the sportsman there are opportunities not only for golf, tennis, squash and bowls, but also for water-skiing, hang-gliding and deep-sea fishing.
25 After a day in the open air, there's lots to do in the evenings, too. There are plenty of discos, the occasional opera or ballet, and summer variety shows in the seafront theatres. For the children, there is a beautiful model village with a
30 complicated railway layout which is remarkably

realistic – especially when the lights are all on at night.

Of course, there's no need to spend your whole holiday in Torquay. Only a short drive
35 away is Dartmoor National Park, where you can walk for miles through dramatic, unspoiled countryside, or picnic by beautiful rivers and streams. Or, nearer to home, you can sail across Tor Bay to the lovely old fishing village of
40 Brixham.

Torquay seems to have something for everyone. But don't take my word for it – come and see for yourself.

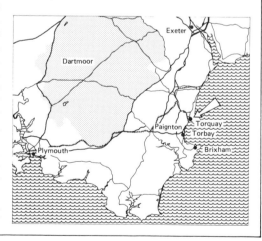

1 Which of these pairs of adjectives best describes Torquay?
  a) sophisticated and expensive   b) crowded and lively   c) remote and beautiful

2 What information does the writer give about:
   a) accommodation in Torquay?
   b) beaches around Torquay?
   c) the cliffs around Torquay?
   d) entertainment in Torquay?
   e) the sea around Torquay?

3 If you *don't* like crowded places, where can you go:
   a) near Torquay?
   b) further away from Torquay?

4 What is special about the model village?

5 What are the following?
   a) coves (line 12)
   b) refreshments (line 15)
   c) deck chairs (line 15)
   d) beach huts (line 16)
   e) variety shows (line 27)

6 Look at the photo. What is it a photo of, and what is there in it?

7 Imagine that you are visiting Torquay for *one* day only. What would you do there? What wouldn't you do? Why?

Writing

Write part of a magazine article describing your town and what visitors can do there.

Unit 1   Summary of language

In this unit you have learnt how to:
– describe and ask about places
– say where things are
– describe and ask about available services
– describe and ask about amenities in towns

KEY POINTS

1 *'There is/are' and 'has/has got'*
   There's a desk in the room.
   There are plenty of cheap hotels in the town.
   Is there a camp site here?

   The room │ **has**
            │ **has got** │ central heating.

   │ **Has** the town **got**
   │ **Does** the town **have** │ a museum?

2 *Location prepositions*
   in, on; above, over, below, under; by, beside, next to; between; opposite; behind,
   in front of.

3 *'Have something done'*
   You can **have** your car wash**ed** at that garage.
   Where can **I have** my coat clean**ed**?

4 *'Non-defining' relative clauses*
   There are night clubs, **which** tend to be rather expensive.
   There are cafés, **where** you can get a cheap cup of coffee.

5 *Vocabulary*
   buildings, rooms and furniture
   services
   amenities in towns

Unit 2   Decisions and intentions

2.1   WILL & GOING TO

Presentation

Four friends have just won £800,000 on the football pools. They celebrate in a restaurant:

Later, a reporter interviews them:

Why do the friends use **I'll** in the restaurant, and **I'm going to** in the interview?

Practice

Work in groups.
1 You have just won £800,000 between you on the football pools. Decide what to do with the money. Use **I think I'll** and **I don't think I'll**.
2 Tell other people in the class about your decisions, using **I'm going to**.

2.2 MAKING DECISIONS   Practice

Decide to do/not to do these things, and add a reason.

Examples: *go for a walk*

| **I think I'll** |
| **Perhaps I'll** | go for a walk. The weather's lovely.
| **Maybe I'll** |

not to have any breakfast

| **I don't think I'll** |
| **Perhaps I won't** | have any breakfast. I'm not very hungry.
| **Maybe I won't** |

Decide:
1 to have a beer
2 not to have a beer
3 to write to your mother
4 not to go out tonight
5 to learn to drive

6 not to have any more to eat
7 not to give up smoking
8 to go swimming
9 to have a party
10 not to invite Jane to your party

Now add a decision to these remarks
1 I'm getting much too fat . . .
2 I'm fed up with my job . . .
3 She seems very friendly . . .
4 I'm a bit tired tonight . . .
5 I really must try and get rid of this cough . . .
6 I hope they're not worried about me . . .
7 I've had enough of these mice running about all over the flat . . .

2.3 CHANGING YOUR MIND   Practice

A: I think I'll get a bus to London.
B: Don't do that. It takes much too long.
A: Does it? Well, in that case I'll go by train instead.
C: Train? Don't be silly – it's terribly expensive.
A: Is it? Oh, well in that case perhaps I'll hitchhike.
D: Hitchhike? . . .

Work in groups. Have similar conversations, and continue as long as you can. Take it in turns to be A.
1 A decides to ask Maria (or Mario) out.
2 A decides to give George a tie for his birthday.
3 A decides to go on holiday to London.
4 A decides to buy a Mercedes.
5 A decides to spend the evening in Anabelle's discotheque.

2.4 INTENTIONS AND PLANS

Presentation

You will hear two students talking about what they are going to do when they leave college. Listen to the tape and answer the questions.

1 What plans has each student got:
   a) for the immediate future?   b) for the more distant future?

2 What exactly does the first student say about:
   a) a holiday?   b) a job?   c) advertising?

3 What exactly does the second student say about:
   a) a restaurant?   b) a temporary job?   c) work and money?   d) a waiter?

4 What isn't (a) the first student (b) the second student completely sure about?

Practice

What do you think the following people are going to do? Talk about their intentions using:

going to	intending to
planning to	thinking of . . . -ing

1 Roger has decided that he doesn't earn enough money.
2 Wendy has decided that her life isn't exciting enough.
3 Grandfather has decided that it's not safe to keep his money under his mattress.
4 The Robinsons are worried because their house is full of valuable antiques.
5 Janet has just bought 100 kilos of cheese.
6 Alex has taken all of his money out of his bank account.

Now what about these people?

2.5 MAKING MONEY

Free practice

Work in pairs.
You and your partner have decided to join together to find a new way of making money (one that is different from your present occupation). Working together, decide what you are going to do. Work out as many details as you can.

Useful expressions

Shall we ...?	Let's ...
Wh- ... shall we ...?	Why don't we ...?

Now form new pairs. Interview each other about what you are planning to do.

Writing

Write a paragraph, explaining what you and your partner are planning to do to make money.

2.6 ARRANGEMENTS

Presentation

Ludwig and Samira are students on a summer course in Cambridge.

Ludwig: Are you coming on the excursion on Saturday?
Samira: What excursion?
Ludwig: To Stratford-on-Avon. We're spending the day there, and then we're seeing a play in the evening.
Samira: Who's going?
Ludwig: Lots of us. They're hiring a coach. Why don't you come too?

Here's the programme. Go through it and say what the students **are doing** on Saturday.

Example They're leaving at quarter to nine.

```
EXCURSION TO STRATFORD-UPON-AVON  Saturday 16 July

0845 Coach departs from Course Centre
1030 Brief stop for coffee at Buckingham
1200 Arrival at Stratford
1230 Lunch booked at Riverside Restaurant
1400 Conducted tour of town
1600-1900 Free  (Please note: participants are advised to
     have an evening meal before the theatre performance.)
1930 Performance of King Lear at Shakespeare Memorial Theatre
2250 Performance ends
2300 Coach departs
0200 Return to Cambridge
```

Practice

It's Saturday morning, and the students are waiting for the coach. Samira has lost her programme, and asks Ludwig some questions about the day's arrangements.

In pairs, act out their conversation. These are Samira's questions:
1 time/leave?
2 stop/see Coventry Cathedral on the way?
3 stop anywhere on the way?
4 when/arrive/Stratford?
5 lunch?
6 visit Shakespeare's birthplace?
7 afternoon?
8 dinner together?
9 which play?
10 start back straight after the performance?
11 stop on the way back?

2.7 YOUR OWN PLANS   Free practice

In groups, talk about your own arrangements and plans for the future. Talk about:
1 after this lesson   4 when this course has finished
2 tonight   5 next year
3 next weekend

If you haven't got any definite plans, make some decisions!

Alan and Jane go to a restaurant, and later Charles joins them. Listen to their conversation.

1 Listen to the first scene again, and write in the missing words.

Waiter: Good evening. Would .... ?

Alan: Er, no. ....

        We'll need ....

Waiter: Ah, ..., perhaps ....

Jane: Thank you.

Waiter: ....

        before .... ?

Alan: Er, no. I ....

        We'll .... Can .... ?

2 a) At the beginning, what do Alan and Jane decide *not* to do?
  b) What does Alan decide *not* to eat?
  c) What does Jane decide *not* to eat?

3 Exactly what does each of the three friends order (a) to eat? (b) to drink?

4 Exactly how does Alan ask about (a) wine? (b) paying?

5 Do you think (a) Jane (b) Charles has been to this restaurant before? Why?

6 The three friends made *two* arrangements yesterday. What were they?

7 Why are they having a meal together?

Unit 2   Summary of language

In this unit you have learnt how to:
– decide to do or not to do things
– come to a decision with somebody else
– talk about intentions and plans
– talk about definite arrangements

KEY POINTS

1 *'I'll' for spontaneous decisions*
   Perhaps/Maybe I'll go to the cinema tonight.
   Perhaps/Maybe I won't go to the cinema tonight.

   I think I'll read that book.
   I don't think I'll read that book.

2 *'Shall we . . .?' and 'Let's . . .'*
   Where **shall we** go this evening?
   Shall we invite Peter to dinner?
   Let's go for a walk.

3 *Verbs expressing intentions and plans*
   I'm going to visit my sister next week.
   They**'re planning to** build an extension to their house.
   She**'s intending to** retire next year.
   I'm thinking of buy**ing** a bicycle.

4 *Present Continuous tense for definite arrangements*
   I'm starting my university course in September. (They've already accepted me.)
   He**'s flying** to Italy on Friday. (He's already booked the ticket.)

Unit 3   Jobs and routine

3.1   JOBS   Presentation and practice

A bus driver is a person
who drives buses.

What do the others do?

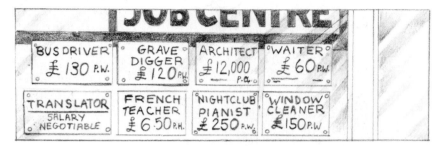

What are these people's jobs?

Example: Fred drives buses.
          He's a bus driver.

1 Janet mends watches.
2 Mac manages a supermarket.
3 Ann sells books.
4 Mandy takes photographs.

5 Jimmy sweeps roads.
6 Richard and Liz act in films.
7 Angela reads the news on television.
8 Chris plays classical music on the guitar.

Now explain what these people do:
a secretary   a nightwatchman
a cashier   a gardener
a mechanic   a receptionist
a plumber   an air hostess

3.2   WHAT'S YOUR JOB?   Practice

A: Where do you work?
B: I work at the local hospital.
A: Oh, so you're a doctor, are you?
B: No, I'm a gardener – I look after the gardens around the hospital.

Have similar conversations, using the ideas below. Each time, say exactly what you
do in your job.

1 police station / policeman? / secretary
2 railway station / ticket collector? / porter
3 supermarket / cashier? / store detective
4 library / librarian? / cleaner
5 ski resort / ski instructor? / ....

6 language school / ....? / ....
7 restaurant / ....? / ....
8 nightclub / ....? / ....
9 airport / ....? / ....

A lot of different people work in these places. How many can you think of for each?

airport   office

nightclub  hotel

theatre 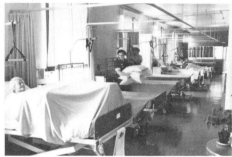 hospital

Choose one of the six workplaces, and one of the jobs that can be done there (e.g. airport – barman). The other people in your group try to guess what your job is. They can only ask about *what you do*.

Example:
A: I work at an airport.   C: Do you carry the passengers' suitcases?
B: Do you fly planes?   A: No, I'm not a porter.
A: No, I'm not a pilot.   D: Do you ....?

3.4 YOUR OWN JOB   Free practice

Work in groups. Find out from the others:
1 what jobs they have
2 what they do exactly
3 what jobs other people in their family have

3.5 DAILY ROUTINE

Presentation

You are asking someone about his/her daily routine. How do you ask about:
1 getting up? (When/What time?)
2 breakfast? (What?)
3 going to work/college? (When? How? How long?)
4 lunch? (When? Where? What?)
5 evenings? (What?)
6 going out? (How often? Where? Who with?)

always	usually	sometimes
never	generally	occasionally
	as a rule	from time to time
	normally	now and again

Put each of these expressions into the sentence below, *in the right place*:

'I have lunch in the office canteen.'

Practice

Work in pairs. Use the language you have practised to:
1 ask about your partner's daily routine
2 talk about your own daily routine

Writing

Now write a short paragraph describing your partner's daily routine.

3.6 PRECISE FREQUENCY

Presentation and practice

The Earth rotates on its axis	once a day.
	every 24 hours.
	365 times a year.

Mrs Smith phones her daughter	once a fortnight.
	every two weeks.
	twice a month.

How often:
1 do leap years occur?
2 do you have elections in your country?
3 does a normal heart beat?
4 do you have an English lesson?
5 do you wash your hair?
6 do you clean your teeth?
7 do you go on holiday?
8 do you have your hair cut?

Practice

> A: I really take good care of my teeth. I brush them twice a day.
> B: That's nothing. I clean my teeth at least three times a day . . . And I go to the dentist every six months.
> A: Is that all? I go to the dentist at least every four months . . . And I use dental floss once a week.
> B: Only once? I . . .

Work in pairs. Have more conversations like this, beginning with the remarks below. Continue each conversation for as long as you can.

1 I like to keep in touch with my parents.
2 I keep my house spotlessly clean.
3 I have a fantastic social life.
4 My boss treats his employees very well.
5 I'm very keen on keeping fit.

3.7 ALL IN A DAY'S WORK: THE PASSIVE

Presentation

Ron Glib is a successful journalist. His newspaper pays him a huge salary, and they publish all his articles. They send him all over the world, and ask him to cover major world events. 'Only I don't like covering big demonstrations,' he says. 'Sometimes the police mistake me for a demonstrator, and arrest me.'

Instead of saying 'His newspaper pays him a huge salary', we can say:

He $\left|\begin{array}{l} \textbf{is} \\ \textbf{gets} \end{array}\right|$ **paid** a huge salary.

What other things happen to Ron Glib? Use these verbs in the Passive:
1 publish
2 send
3 ask
4 mistake
5 arrest

Practice

Now talk about these people, using the Passive. What good and bad things do you think happen to them?
1 a pop star
2 a doctor
3 a policeman
4 a politician
5 you

3.8   A LIFE IN THE DAY OF...   Reading

In this passage, Janet Thompson and Warren Maxwell describe a typical working day.

Janet: The alarm goes off at 4.30. I get up and go and wake Warren. Then I go downstairs, make some tea, and take a cup up to Warren. He has lived with us ever since he came over here from New Zealand ten years ago, and we are like brother and sister now.

Warren: It takes us about 45 minutes to wake up and get ready. We always leave the house at exactly a quarter past five. I drive us in Janet's dad's car, and we arrive at the ice rink at exactly twenty past five. The cleaner arrives just in time to let us in. We get changed and we're on the ice by twenty to six.

Janet: At a quarter past eight, we get changed and go off for breakfast in a little Italian café round the corner. I have toast and tea, and Warren usually has something like sausages, eggs and tea. We both eat terribly fattening foods, but neither of us seems to get fat, which is very lucky. At nine, we go back to the rink and work through until twelve. Then we go for a run in Hyde Park for about half an hour.

Warren: Yes, it's quite nice in the park, except when you get chased by dogs. After our run we just buy a sandwich and eat it at work. Janet works in a department store and I work in a betting office. They're very good to us: they let us have as much time off as we need for skating – although of course we don't get paid. In the evening we meet up again just before six in the Dance Centre, for a modern dance class. We get back to Janet's parents' flat by about eight, have dinner and a bath and go straight to bed. Although it's a very long day for us, I never really feel we are missing out on anything. We sometimes see friends at weekends: they're married, they've got ordinary jobs and they go out in the evenings, but they're envious of what we do, rather than the other way round.

(from *The Sunday Times* (adapted))

1 a)   What is Janet and Warren's main occupation?
  b)   What do they do to earn a living?

2 Choose the correct answer. Are they:
  a)   married?
  b)   boyfriend and girlfriend?
  c)   brother and sister?
  d)   friends?

3 a)   Where do Janet and Warren live?
  b)   Why do you think they live together?

4 Exactly when do they skate?

5 What problems are involved in:
  a)   running in Hyde Park?
  b)   taking time off work?

6 Write T (true) or F (false) against these statements:
  a)   The rink is closed when they arrive.
  b)   They live a well-organised life.
  c)   They don't think they have enough free time.
  d)   Their employers let them skate during working hours.
  e)   They envy their friends.

7 Make brief notes about Janet and Warren's daily routine. Use these times as a guide:

4.30	12.00
5.15	12.30
5.20	1.00–5.30?
5.40	6.00
8.15	8.00
9.00	9.00?

Work in groups of three.

Student A: You are going to interview Janet and Warren. Ask them questions about their daily routine, and ask anything else you like (e.g. how they feel about their life; how they met; what they like about skating; their future plans).

Students B and C: You are Janet and Warren. Using your notes, answer the interviewer's questions about your daily routine. When you are asked about other things, invent suitable answers.

Unit 3   *Summary of language*

In this unit you have learnt how to:
– describe people's jobs
– talk and ask about daily routine
– talk and ask about regular events

KEY POINTS

1 *Compound noun phrases*
He teaches English.
He's an **English teacher**.

He mends shoes.
He's a **shoe mender**.

2 *Present Simple question forms*
What time do you **go** to work?
How often do you **wash** your hair?

3 *Adverbs and phrases expressing general frequency*
I **usually** get up at 7 o'clock, but **occasionally** I get up later.
As a rule, I get up at 7 o'clock.
I get up at 7 o'clock **as a rule**.

4 *Phrases expressing precise frequency*
He visits his aunt **three times a week**.
They send us a gas bill **every three months**.
I go swimming **once a week**.

5 *Present Simple Passive with 'be' or 'get'*
They pay the workers once a month.

The workers | are / get | **paid** once a month.

Sometimes people mistake him for his brother.

Sometimes he | is / gets | **mistaken** for his brother.

6 *Vocabulary*
jobs and places of work

Unit 4 Direction

4.1 PREPOSITIONS OF DIRECTION   Presentation

What possible directions can you go in if you are:

1 in a street?   5 near a house?
2 by a low wall?   6 in a field?
3 by a bed?   7 standing near a tunnel?
4 a fly on a wall?   8 near two trees?

Now write appropriate prepositions in the gaps.

1 When the bull began to run .... me, I jumped .... the fence .... the next field.

2 He took two books .... the shelf. He put one of them .... the table, and the other one .... his briefcase.

3 She ran .... the corridor, and .... the stairs into the basement.

4 His bullet whistled .... my ear, so I shot him right .... the eyes.

5 He came .... her, and put his arm .... her waist.

6 The prisoner jumped .... the window, ran .... the street, and jumped .... a car that was waiting for him on the other side.

7 Looking .... the microscope, she saw the two cells separate and move slowly .... each other.

8 They couldn't get .... the high wall, so they dug a tunnel .... it.

4.2 WHERE DO THEY GO? Practice

Look at the three pictures below, and say:

1 exactly where the road goes
2 exactly where the burglar went, from the evidence of his footprints in the snow
3 exactly what the soldier has to do to complete the assault course

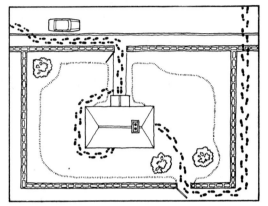

4.3 HOW DO YOU DO IT? Practice

Example: *You've got a coconut, a screwdriver and a cup. How do you get the milk out?*

First you push the screwdriver into the end of the coconut and make two holes. Then you pour the milk out of the coconut through one of the holes into the cup.

In the same way, say how to do these things. Be as precise as possible.

1 You've got a rope and a rock. How do you anchor your boat?

2 You've got a matchbox, two needles, a candle, and a knife. How do you make a model car?

3 You've got a rope, a sheet and six pencils. How do you make a tent?

4 You've got a bottle of beer and some jam. How do you make a trap for wasps?

5 You're walking along a road and you come to a crossroads. There's a four-way signpost, but it has come out of its hole and is lying at the side of the road. The name of the place you want to go to is written on one of the arms of the signpost. How do you find which road to take?

Here is an incomplete picture of a burglar in a house.
Where are the following in the picture?

1 a soda siphon
2 a pulley
3 a horn
4 a weight
5 a roller

Work in pairs.

Student A: Your partner will describe the missing parts of the picture. As you listen, draw them in.

Student B: Turn to page 181 and look at the complete picture. Don't show it to your partner! Describe for him/her exactly where the pieces of string *go*, and what they are *tied to*.

Now check your results.

From your completed pictures, describe exactly what happens when the burglar picks up the watch.

The plan shows a number of destinations, marked A–L.

1 To which destinations do these directions take you?
   a) Go down this road and **take the** third **turning on the** right.
   b) You go straight along this road and **take the** second **turning on the** left.

2 Now give similar directions to destinations B, G and E.

3 To which destinations do these directions take you?
   a) You keep straight on **until you get to** the end of the road. Then you **turn** left.
   b) Go along this road **as far as** the Post Office, and then **turn** right.
   c) Go straight down this road and **turn** left **at the** supermarket.

4 Now give similar directions to destinations I, C and K.

5 To which destinations do these directions take you?
   a) Keep straight on **past** the school **and then take the first turning on the** right.
   b) You go down this road and **take the first turning on the** right **after** the hotel.

6 Now give similar directions to destinations J, G and C.

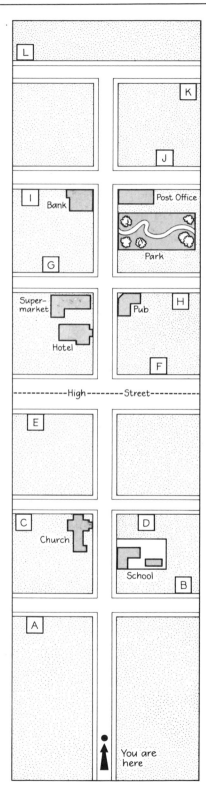

4.6 FINDING YOUR WAY   Practice

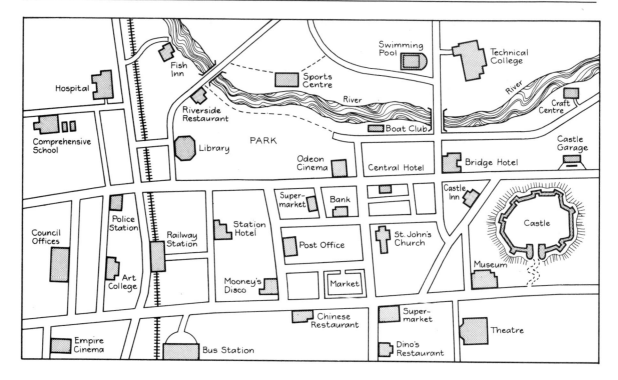

Work in pairs. You are at the bus station. Ask each other the way to:

1 the castle   4 the bank
2 the library   5 the comprehensive school
3 the boat club   6 the swimming pool

Student A begins: **Excuse me,** | **how do I get to . . . ?**
| **can you tell me the way to . . . ?**

Student B finishes: **You'll see the . . . on your** | **left.**
| **right.**

Now imagine you are somewhere else on the map. Choose a place you want to go to, and ask your partner how to get there.

4.7 YOUR OWN AREA   Free practice

Work in groups. Tell each other how to get to these places, from where you are now.

1 the nearest Post Office
2 the nearest station
3 the nearest supermarket
4 your house
5 anywhere else you like

You will hear a woman describe two ways of making puppets, and tell the story of
how she once gave a puppet show.

1 Before you listen,
   a) make sure you know the meaning of the following words and expressions:

      to embroider   sleeve
      to stuff   elastic band
      cardboard tube   frame

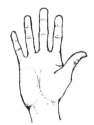

   b) mark the following on the hand on the right:
      thumb
      forefinger
      middle finger
      wrist

2 Listen to what the woman says about the first way of making a puppet.
   a) How do you make the *head*? the *hair*? the *eyes*?
   b) Where do you put the cardboard tube? Why?
   c) How is the puppet's dress different from an ordinary doll's dress?
   d) How exactly do you put the puppet on your hand?

3 Listen to what she says about the second way of making a puppet.
   a) Make a list of *all* the materials you need, and what each thing is for.

Material	What it's for
matchbox cover	the puppet's head
paper	

   b) Explain how you put the puppet together on your hand. Begin 'You take the
      handkerchief, and you put it . . .'

4 Listen to the story about the puppet show she gave in Cornwall.
   a) What kind of puppets did she use?
   b) How did she make her theatre?
   c) How did she find an audience?

Make a matchbox puppet.

Unit 4   Summary of language

In this unit you have learnt how to:
– say what direction things and people move in
– give instructions for making and doing things
– give street directions

1 *Prepositions of direction*
   in(to), out of;
   on(to), off;
   up to, towards, away from;
   up, down;
   along, through, between;
   across, round, past, over, under.

2 *Expressing sequence in giving instructions*
   First you put a paper cup under the tap. **After that you** put your money in the machine, **and then you** press the button . . .

3 *Expressions for giving street directions*
   Turn **left/right**.
   Take the first turning **on your left/on your right**.
   | **Keep** | **straight on** along this road.
   | **Go** |

Activities

ROOM TO LET

A student sees this advertisement
in a newsagent's window, and
phones the owner.

> ROOM TO LET
> Large bed-sitter
> 16 Bryants Lane
> phone 647-0814   £30 p.w.

Student: Phone the owner, and:
    1 ask him/her to describe the room
    2 ask for any more information you need
    3 decide to go and see it
    4 ask how to get there

Owner: When the student phones you:
    1 describe the room
    2 answer any more questions about it
    3 ask if he/she is coming to see the room
    4 tell him/her how to get there

COMPOSITION

Write a short magazine article (100–150 words), entitled 'A day in the life of (your
name)'. Include information about:

your job	people you come into contact with
the work you do	things that often happen to you
breaks for meals	travel

SITUATIONS

1 You want to go swimming, but a friend tells you the pool's closed. Decide to do
something else.
2 Someone asks you the way to the nearest bank. Give directions.
3 Explain the weekly routine of your English classes to a new student.
4 Explain to someone how to get the milk out of a coconut.
5 You're in a strange town and your bicycle has a puncture. Ask a passer-by about a
place that will repair it.
6 Someone you meet at a party asks you to recommend a good place to spend an
evening in your town. What do you say to them?

Unit 5   Past events

5.1   RELATING PAST EVENTS

Presentation

You will hear an interview in which a famous writer and film maker talks about some of the events in his life.

Listen to the interview and answer these questions:

What did the writer do:
1 before he went to Indonesia?
2 while he was in Indonesia?
3 after he came back from Indonesia?
4 three years later?
5 two years after he published *The Cold Earth*?

Now listen again and write each event by its date.

1959	left school
1960	
1961	
1965	
1969	
1970	
1973	
1975	
1977	
1978	

Practice

1 The writer left school in 1959. A year | later / after that | he wrote his first novel. A year | later / after that | he . . .

Go through the other events in the writer's life in the same way.

2 (A year) **after** | **leaving** school | the writer wrote his first novel.
   | **he left** school |

   (A year) **after** | **writing** his first novel, | he . . .
   | **he wrote** his first novel, |

Go through the other events in the writer's life in the same way.

5.2 BEFORE, AFTER & WHILE   Practice

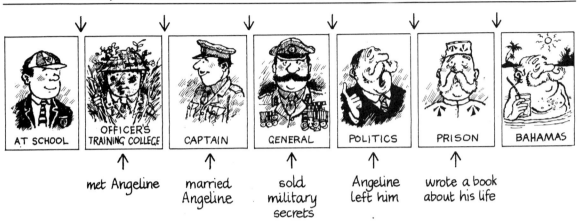

1 The pictures show seven periods in Geoffrey's life.
   Look at the arrows *above* the pictures. What events does each point to?
2 The arrows *below* the pictures show other events in his life.
   In groups, ask and answer questions about when each happened.
   Example A: When did he meet Angeline?
             B: He met her **before** he became a captain.
             C: He met her **after** he went to college.
             D: He met her **while** he was at college.

5.3 FIRST EXPERIENCES   Practice

   A: When did you learn to drive?
   B: I learnt to drive **when** I was 18. How about you?
   A: | I learnt to drive **when** I was 16. |
      | I **didn't** learn to drive **till** I was 20. |

Work in pairs. Have similar conversations.
When did you:
1 learn to swim?   5 start learning English?
2 first wear make-up?   6 smoke your first cigarette?
3 first go abroad?   7 first fly in an aeroplane?
4 start earning money?   8 first fall in love?

Now continue with your own ideas.

5.4 LIFE STORY   Writing

Look at your notes in 5.1. From your notes, write the story of the writer's life. Use appropriate expressions you have learnt to link the events together. Begin like this:

'David Manning was born in London in 1942, and attended Westminster School for Boys ...'

5.5 PAST TIMES

Presentation

All of the expressions below are used to talk about past time. Which of them are used with (a) at? (b) on? (c) in? (d) no preposition?

4 o'clock	Tuesday, 14 May	the 1920s
yesterday	three weeks ago	the turn of the century
Tuesday	the end of May	Victorian times
last Tuesday	Christmas	the 19th century
Tuesday morning	the summer	the Middle Ages
14 May	last summer	1,000 years ago
May	1945	

Practice

Work in groups. Ask and answer questions about the past. Use these ideas:

get up?	buy house/flat?
be born?	war begin/end?
finish Unit 3?	Shakespeare/write?
term begin?	America/independent?
start/job?	wear/miniskirts?
jazz/popular?	

5.6 PAST EVENTS: THE PASSIVE

Presentation and practice

ELGAR: Symphony No. 1 in A Flat, Op. 55
London Philharmonic Orchestra
GEORG SOLTI
(SXL 6569)
(1972) Decca

This is an entry in a record catalogue. It tells you that the symphony was composed by Elgar, that the orchestra was conducted by Georg Solti, and that the record was made in 1972. What else does it tell you?

Now look at these other pieces of information, and say:
1 where you might find them
2 what they tell you – use the Passive in your answer

SUNFLOWERS by Van Gogh

Nuits St Georges 1975

BIRTHPLACE OF WILLIAM SHAKESPEARE 1564 – 1616

Roman Earrings (circa 100 AD)

TO THE UNKNOWN SOLDIER 1914 – 1918

ANNA KARENINA English translation by Rosemary Edmonds

PLUM TOMATOES Produce of Italy

WILLIAMSON COLLEGE Founder: Lord Williamson

CAXTON'S PRINTING PRESS (1476)

Doff & Jones *Feelings* (CUP 1980)

Writing

Work in groups. Look at the pictures below, which show the history of Cranmore Castle.
1 Say what happened at each stage of its history.
2 Write a history of Cranmore Castle. Use the information in the pictures, and add details of your own.
   Begin like this:
   'Cranmore Castle was built in the 15th century by John, Duke of Cranmore . . .'

15th Century   1633   1660s   18th Century

1920s   1950   1964   1968

Can you answer these questions?
1 What happened in Rome on 14 March 44 BC?
2 Who were the following discovered by?
   a) penicillin
   b) North America
   Can you say when?
3 Who were the Pyramids built by, and when?
4 When:
   a) did the first man step on the moon?
   b) did the first aeroplane fly?
   c) was a woman elected Prime Minister of Britain?

Now write down three 'quiz' questions of your own about the past.

In groups, ask each other your questions.

Now choose the three best questions in your group, and ask the rest of the class these questions.

5.8   FAMOUS LIVES

Reading

Work in three groups.
1 Read your own passage, and decide who it is about.
2 Practise retelling the life story without looking at the passage.
3 Form new groups (one A, one B and one C). Tell the others the story, so that they can guess who it is about.

Group A: He was born in the United States at the turn of the century. As a young man, he was very active, and spent a lot of time hunting and fishing. He started working as a journalist, but during the First World War he was an ambulance driver in Italy, where he was badly wounded in 1917. After fighting in the Spanish Civil War, he worked as an army correspondent until 1945, when he went to live in Cuba. In 1954 he won a Nobel Prize. He stayed in Cuba until the Castro Revolution in 1959, and then returned to live in the United States. He was married four times, and later in his life became physically and mentally ill. On 2 July 1961, he committed suicide.

Group B: She was born into a wealthy family in Philadelphia in 1930, and she had her first part on the stage when she was 12 years old. Five years later, after visiting Europe with her family, she was admitted to the American Academy of Dramatic Arts in New York. While she was there she did some modelling and TV commercials to earn some extra money. She first appeared on Broadway in 1949. In 1951, after appearing in several plays on stage and on TV, she played the hero's wife in the film *High Noon*. She then had star roles in two Alfred Hitchcock films, and later won an Oscar for her role in *The Country Girl*. In April 1956 she left Hollywood and got married. She had a daughter in 1957, followed by a son 14 months later, and another daughter in 1965. She lived in Monaco until her death in 1982.

Group C: She was born in September 1890 in Torquay, in the southwest of England. She married in 1914, just before the beginning of the First World War. During the War, she worked first as a nurse, and then in a hospital dispensary, where she learnt all about drugs and poisons. Her husband returned from France at the end of the War, and they had a daughter in 1919. Eight years later, in 1927, she got divorced, and after two or three years' work, she went on holiday to Baghdad, where she joined a British archaeological expedition. There she met her second husband: they travelled back to England together on the Orient Express, and got married in September 1930. They went on two more archaeological expeditions in Syria, and during the Second World War she again worked in a dispensary. After more travels to the Middle East in 1947 and 1949, she and her husband moved back to the southwest of England, where she worked until her death in 1976. In 1971 she was made a Dame of the British Empire.

Writing

Write a similar paragraph about yourself.

Unit 5   Summary of language

In this unit you have learnt how to:
– relate and ask about past events
– say when events happened
– tell the history of people and places

KEY POINTS

1 *'Sequence' expressions*

He left university in 1960. A year | **later** / **after that** | he became a teacher.

A year **after** | **leaving** / **he left** | university, he became a teacher.

He became a millionaire
- **after** he went to Australia.
- **when/while** he was in Australia.
- **before** he left Australia.

He didn't become a millionaire **till/until** he went to Australia.

2 *Past Simple tense: negatives and questions*
I met Susan in 1950.
I **didn't** meet Susan till 1950.
When **did** you meet Susan?

3 *Time expressions with and without prepositions*
at 6 p.m.   at Easter
on Sunday evening   on 6 July
in 1960   in September   in the autumn   in Roman times
last Monday   yesterday   five years ago

4 *Past Simple Passive*
They built the house in the 19th century.
The house **was built** in the 19th century.

Cervantes wrote *Don Quixote*.
Don Quixote **was written** by Cervantes.

Unit 6 Talking about now

6.1 USES OF THE PRESENT CONTINUOUS   Presentation

Read these three passages, each of which uses the Present Continuous.

A

... And now the Royal Coach is turning into Parliament Square. There are thousands of people waiting in the Square, and everyone is standing on tiptoe, trying to catch a glimpse of the Royal Family. The children are all waving their Union Jacks ... Now the coach is stopping and the Queen is getting out. She's wearing ...

B

... There are two continuing reasons for the danger of flooding. These are that London is slowly sinking and that the tides in general are rising. Not only is central London sinking on its bed of clay, but over the centuries Britain itself is tilting. Scotland and the northwest are rising, and southeastern England is gradually dipping at a rate of one foot every hundred years ...

C

Having a lovely time in London. We're eating in some very expensive restaurants, and meeting lots of interesting people. I'm spending most of my time walking around central London and visiting museums. The Cup Final's tomorrow, so everyone's talking about football ...

All the passages are talking about 'now'. In what ways are they different?

6.2 WHAT ARE THEY DOING?   Practice

A: Hello, Suntours Ltd. Can I help you?
B: Yes, I'd like to speak to the Manager, please.
A: I'm afraid he's not available at the moment. He's attending a meeting.
B: Oh. Could I speak to his secretary, then?
A: I'm afraid she's not available, either. She's ...

Have conversations like this, using these ideas:

1 *Murphie's Garage*: Mr Murphie; the chief mechanic.
2 *Ogilvie, Blunt & Partners (Solicitors)*: Mr Ogilvy; Mr Blunt.
3 *University Physics Dept*: Dr Lloyd; Dr Lloyd's secretary.
4 *The Regency School of English*: the Director; the Information Officer.
5 *Buckingham Palace*: the Queen; the Duke of Edinburgh; Prince Charles.

6.3 SEE FOR YOURSELF

Presentation

Example: *Somebody's watching us.*
　　　　　There's somebody **watching** us.
　　　　　We're **being watched.**

Change these sentences in the same way:
1 Someone's following us.
2 Some men are pulling down the house.
3 Another car's overtaking us.
4 Someone's looking after the children.
5 Two policemen are questioning the man.

6 A man's feeding the tigers.
7 Nobody's using the car today.
8 Nobody's guarding the prisoner.
9 Is anybody making the tea?
10 Is anyone using this room?

Practice

Add an explanation to each of the remarks below, saying *what is happening.*
Examples　Don't go out in your sandals: It's pouring with rain.
　　　　　Could you answer the door: There's someone ringing the bell.
　　　　　Keep your head down: We're being shot at.

1 Don't switch the radio off:
2 You'd better hurry up and eat that ice cream:
3 We need to have our roof repaired:
4 Pass me a paper handkerchief:

5 I'm afraid you can't use that room just now:
6 You should put some suntan oil on your back:
7 There's no need to worry about the children:
8 Quick, darling, hide in the wardrobe:

6.4 DESCRIBE AND CHOOSE　Practice

Work in pairs.
Student A: Choose *one* of the five pictures below. Describe it to B, by saying *only* what is happening, what people are doing, etc. B will guess which picture you are describing.
Student B: Listen to A's description. When you think you know which picture he or she is describing, check your guess by asking some questions.

6.5 LONG-TERM CHANGES   Free practice

Discuss the topics below. Say what changes are taking place, and, if you can, explain why.

1 Venice
2 the sun
3 the world's fuel resources
4 the Sahara Desert

5 life expectancy
6 the Mediterranean Sea
7 the population of the world

6.6 CURRENT ACTIVITIES   Practice

A: What do you do?
B: I'm a film producer. I make documentary films.

A: What are you | making / working on | at the moment?

B: I'm making a documentary about horse racing.

Have more conversations like this. You're talking to:

1 a writer   3 a painter   5 a detective
2 an architect   4 a composer   6 a journalist

Talk to other students. Find out the kind of things they're doing these days.

Read these sentences, which describe present situations:

SECTION A
1 Their flat is being completely modernised:
2 Miss World is being given V.I.P. treatment:
3 The war's causing terrible suffering:
4 My car's still at the garage:
5 The college has been without electricity for a week now:
6 Christmas is coming:
7 The family next door is being closely watched:

Now read these sentences, which continue the sentences in section A and give more details. Each sentence in section A has *two* continuation sentences.

SECTION B
... they're putting up coloured lights in the High Street.
... people are taking her out to nightclubs.
... they're taking out all the old fireplaces.
... they're sending most students home at 5 o'clock.
... they're fitting a new exhaust pipe.
... they're holding evening classes by gas light.
... troops are destroying the crops.
... they're tapping their telephone.
... they're tightening the brakes.
... they're selling Christmas trees in all the shops.
... they're watching the house from across the street.
... everyone's buying her bouquets of roses.
... the invading army is burning down all the villages.
... they're putting in central heating.

1 Match the sentences in section A with the continuations in section B.

2 Read them out, changing the continuation sentences into the Passive.
   Example Their flat is being completely modernised: all the old fireplaces are being taken out and central heating is being put in.

6.8 WHAT'S GOING ON?

Free practice

Here is part of a letter, in which the writer is giving some current news:

We're having very hot weather at the moment.
Everyone is living out of doors. There are people
sunbathing in all the parks. The girls are all wearing
their summer dresses. People are queueing to get into
the swimming pool. And the ice cream sellers are
making a fortune.

Work in groups. Look at the sentences below. How might they continue?

1 I've decided to go on a diet ...
2 There's a water shortage at the moment ...
3 I'm very short of money at the moment ...
4 Spring is almost here ...

Writing

Choose two of the topics you discussed, and develop them into paragraphs.

6.9 A TELEPHONE CALL

Listening

Listen to the telephone conversation between Sue and Mike and answer the questions.

1 Choose the correct answers, (a) or (b).

Sue is on holiday in | (a) Spain / (b) England | with her | (a) sister. / (b) boyfriend. | She is ringing up her | (a) boyfriend, / (b) brother, | Mike, because it's | (a) her / (b) his | birthday. Mike has stayed at home because | (a) he's ill. / (b) he's working. | When she phones, he is just | (a) having breakfast. / (b) making coffee.

2 What is the weather like in England? *Rainy.*
3 What does Sue mean when she says:
   a) 'It's absolutely boiling!' *hot*
   b) 'I'm living in my bikini!' *sun bath..*
4 Why is she sending Mike a postcard? *She want to let him know what Spain looks like.*
5 What does Sue say people are doing where she is? *Sun bathing*
6 What does Mike say people are doing where he is? *Complaining the awful summer*
7 What do you think Mike does for a living?

⟫⟶

41

8 Listen to the last part of the conversation and fill in the missing words.

Sue: Oh dear, still, I expect ....

How's it going?

Mike: Oh, fine. I'm .... Actually, at this

very moment .... and ....

Good God, that .... Can you .... ?

The kettle .... Just a tick.

Sue Hey, Mike, don't go .... This ....

.... I'll *ring you for another day* , OK?

Writing

Some of the things Sue says in the conversation could also be written on a postcard. Write down as many as you can.
Using these expressions, write the postcard Sue might have sent to Mike. Add any details you like.

Unit 6   Summary of language

In this unit you have learnt how to:
– talk about what is happening at the moment
– talk about long-term changes in progress
– talk about current activities
– describe what is happening in pictures

KEY POINTS

1 *Present Continuous tense*
She's hav**ing** a bath at the moment.
The sun **is** gradually cool**ing** down.
A lot of people **are** wear**ing** white jeans this year.

2 *There + Present Continuous*
There are some men mend**ing** the road.
Look – **there's** someone stand**ing** outside the window.
Is there anyone sitt**ing** here?

3 *Present Continuous Passive*
Someone's recording our voices.   They are completely reorganising the office.
Our voices **are being** recorded.   The office **is being** completely reorganis**ed**.

Activities

INTERVIEWING FAMOUS PEOPLE

Work in groups. Take it in turns to be student A.

Student A: Imagine that you are a famous person. (Choose someone you
                        know a lot about.) Answer the others' questions about your
                        life. After the interview they will try to guess who you are.
Students B, C and D: Student A is a famous person. Interview him/her about his/her
                        life. Ask about:
                        1 his/her past life and career
                        2 what he/she does
                        3 what he/she is doing at the moment

After the interview, try to guess who he/she is.

COMPOSITION

Write 100–150 words on one of these topics:

1 Imagine that, 50 years from now, someone in your class is very famous. Write an
   account of his/her life.
2 Write an account of the most important events in your country's history, and when
   they happened.

Unit 7   Requests and offers

7.1   ASKING PEOPLE TO DO THINGS

Presentation

1 Why does the speaker ask for help in a different way in each picture?
2 In what *other* situations might you say 'I don't suppose you could help me get the washing in, could you?'

Practice

Work in pairs.
Student A: You are staying at your friend's house for the weekend. At various times you make the requests below. Choose the most appropriate way of asking, from the expressions in the box.
Student B: Reply to each request in any way you like. If you refuse, give a *reason*.

Could you . . . ?	Would you mind . . . -ing . . . ?	I don't suppose you could
Would you . . . ?	Do you think you could . . . ?	. . ., could you?
. . ., could you?		Do you think you could
. . ., would you?		possibly . . . ?

A wants B to:

1 lend him his bike
2 bring him breakfast in bed
3 wake him up in the morning
4 pass him the newspaper
5 give him a spare front door key
6 lend him his Alfa Romeo
7 lend him his best suit
8 switch on the water heater
9 put an extra blanket on his bed
10 give him a lift to the station

Now *report* the conversations you have had, as in the example.

Example I **asked** her **to** help me get the washing in, | and | she **agreed.**
she **said** she **would.** |
| but | she **refused.**
she **wouldn't.** |

7.2 GETTING PEOPLE TO STOP   Presentation and practice

A: | Do you think you could stop
Would you mind not | whistling? – I'm trying to write an essay.

B: Oh, I'm sorry. | I thought you were in the other room.
I didn't realise you were working. |

Have more conversations like this, using the prompts below. A must make up a
reason why he wants B to stop, and B must make up an *apology*.

B keeps:
1 tapping his/her foot
2 blowing smoke in your face
3 speaking English
4 snoring
5 humming Beethoven symphonies
6 interrupting you
7 filling your glass with wine

7.3 REQUEST NOTES   Writing

Rita,
    I've got 'flu. Would you mind taking my class this afternoon? We're in Room 302. We've just started Unit 7.   John.

Mandy,
    John wants me to take his class this afternoon but I can't because I'm having my eyes tested. Do you think you could take the class instead? It's in Room 302 at 3.15, and they've just started Unit 7,   Rita

Work in pairs.
Choose one of the situations below and write a note for it.
Pass your note to another pair.
Look at the note you have received. You can't help. Write a note to a third person,
explaining the situation, and asking him/her to help instead.

1 You can't go to work tomorrow. Write a
note for your secretary.
2 You lent a book to a friend. Write a note
asking him/her to bring it back this
evening.
3 You are going to stay out late, and you
haven't got a key. Leave a note for your
brother.
4 You are going away on holiday. Leave a
note for your next-door neighbour.

7.4 ASKING FOR PERMISSION

Presentation and practice

A driver has just picked up a hitchhiker. The hitchhiker asks for permission to do two things:

| **Do you mind** / **Is it all right** | if I leave my rucksack on the back seat? |

| **Would you mind** / **Would it be all right** | if I took off my shoes? |

1 What other requests does the hitchhiker make? Use the ideas below.
   a) window   d) radio
   b) map   e) sleep
   c) sandwiches   f) drive

2 What requests for permission might you make in these situations?
   a) You're having an interview for a job.
   b) You're staying at a small hotel.
   c) You're camping in a farmer's field.

Practice

> Hitchhiker: Is it all right if I leave my rucksack on the back seat?
> Driver: Yes, of course. Go ahead.
> Hitchhiker: And ... er ... would you mind if I took off my shoes? My feet are killing me.
> Driver: Well, I'd rather you didn't. It's a rather hot day.

In pairs, have similar conversations, for the situations below. Each time, you must make up the second request yourself.
1 You're staying at your uncle's house. You want to invite some friends over.
2 You're at a friend's house. You want to borrow a record.
3 You're at a party. You want to get some ice from the fridge.
4 You're in your boss's office. You want to take your jacket off.

Now *report* the conversations you have had, as in the example.

Example He **asked** the driver **if** he **could** | leave his rucksack on the seat. / take off his shoes. |

The driver | **let** him leave his rucksack on the seat. / **wouldn't let** him take off his shoes. |

Presentation

Look at the pictures below. What offers do you think the people are making?

Practice

You have a guest for the weekend. You want to be a good host, so instead of waiting for him to ask for things, you guess what he wants and make offers. What do you say if:

1 he looks thirsty?
2 it's time for the news, and he's looking at the radio?
3 he looks hot?
4 he's left his suitcase at the station?
5 he looks bored?

6 he hasn't seen much of your town?
7 he's hot and tired after his journey?
8 he doesn't know how to operate the record-player?
9 he's leaving, and it's a long way to the station?

7.6 REPORTING OFFERS

Presentation

You will hear a conversation between Henry and Tony. Listen to the tape and answer the questions.

1 Who are Henry and Tony, and where do you think they are?
2 Why isn't Tony happy?
3 How does Henry help?
4 What does Tony decide to do?
5 What does Henry promise to do, and why?
6 What do you think Henry really intends to do?
7 During the conversation, Henry makes *three* offers. Report them, using the expressions below.
  a) **He offers . . .**   b) **He offers to . . .**   c) **He offers to let . . .**

Practice

Here are some things that someone said to you. Report each one, beginning 'She offered . . .'

1 Would you like a sandwich?
2 You can drive if you like.
3 Shall I carry it for you?
4 Would you like me to help you?
5 Would you like to sit down?
6 I've finished. Do you want to read it?
7 Would you like the day off tomorrow?
8 I'll deliver it if you like.
9 Would you like to work for us?
10 I've got lots of money, if you're short.

Writing

Decide exactly what happened after Tony left the office. Imagine you are *either* Henry *or* Tony. Tell a friend what happened during the conversation and afterwards.

7.7 PROBLEMS   Free practice

Work in threes.

Student A: Tell B that he/she has a problem.
Student B: Try to ask for help *before* C offers to help you.
Student C: Try to offer to help B *before* he/she asks for help.

Examples A: You've got a headache.
      B tries to say: 'Could you get me an aspirin?' before C says: 'Would you like an aspirin?'
    A: Your car's broken down.
      B tries to say: 'Would you mind if I used your car?' before C says: 'I'll lend you my car if you like.'

48

Reading

Read the passage below, and answer the questions.

No just a tonic for me yes quite sure no really I'd rather not if you don't mind you see the way I look at it is this I've given my old liver a bit of a hard time these last thirty years and I suddenly woke up one evening and asked myself do I really need it no I don't mind you having one God knows how much of that stuff I've poured down my throat if I had a penny for every Scotch I've drunk I'd be a rich man today I tell you no I don't miss it at all it's not so much will-power as common sense isn't it have you ever seen that thing they do with a coin and a bottle of gin it's a bit of an eye opener oh all right just to be sociable but just a small one if you insist . . .

(from *Private Eye* (adapted))

1 What is the man being offered?
2 What, in general, is he telling the other person?
3 Explain what he means when he says:
   a) I've given my old liver a bit of a hard time.
   b) God knows how much of that stuff I've poured down my throat.
   c) I suddenly woke up one evening.
   d) It's a bit of an eye opener.
4 Give an example of your own of (a) willpower (b) common sense.
5 What is the man *doing* when he says 'Oh all right, just to be sociable'? Why does he say that?
6 What do you think is 'that thing they do with a coin and a bottle of gin'?
7 a) Mark the places where the person holding the tray speaks (or tries to speak).
   b) What do you think she says?
8 In what ways is the man a 'bore'?

Writing

Write the passage out as a *conversation* with the person holding the tray, and include punctuation.

Unit 7 Summary of language

In this unit you have learnt how to:
– ask people to do and not to do things
– ask permission to do things
– offer to do things and to let people do things
– report requests and offers

KEY POINTS

1 *Appropriate structures for requests*
   Could you make a cup of coffee?
   Lend me a pound, **would you**?
   | **Do you think you could** lend me
   | **Would you mind** lending me   your bicycle?
   I don't suppose you could look after my dog for a week, **could you**?

2 *'Negative' requests*
   Do you think you could **stop** staring at me?
   Would you mind **not** staring at me?

3 *Appropriate requests for permission*
   Do you mind if I open the window?
   Would it be all right if I opened all the windows?

4 *Reporting requests and responses*
   I **asked** him **to** come with me, but he **refused**.
   I **asked** her **if I could** use the kitchen.
   They **let** me go home early.

5 *Offers and offers of permission*
   Would you like a cup of tea?

   Would you like me to go to the bank for you?
   I'll go to the bank for you **if you like**.

   Would you like to spend the night here?
   You can spend the night here **if you like**.

6 *Reporting offers*
   She **offered me** a cup of tea.
   She **offered to** go to the bank for me.
   She **offered to let me** spend the night at her house.

Unit 8   Recent actions and activities

8.1   MAKING PREPARATIONS

Presentation

Ronnie has had a busy day. He's been making a
lot of preparations. He woke up early, went to
the Rent-a-car office, and hired a new car. Then,
after a quick breakfast, he went to John's
house, borrowed a long ladder, which he
put on the roof of the car, and drove to work.

During his coffee break, he made a copy of
his birth certificate, and before he had lunch
he visited the bank and closed his account.
After lunch, he just had time to rush into the
travel agent's and book a hotel room.

Then on his way home from work he bought three bottles of champagne. As soon
as he got home, he rushed upstairs and packed all his clothes. 'That's it,' he said to
himself. 'I've done everything!'

Now Ronnie's talking on the telephone. 'Julia? Everything's ready. I'll be round for
you at midnight . . .'

Ronnie has done seven important things today. What are they?

Practice

Ronnie and Julia are still on the phone. Julia wants to make sure that Ronnie really
has done everything.

Julia: **Have** you **borrowed** the ladder?
Ronnie: Yes, I have.
Julia: Are you sure, Ronnie?

Ronnie: Yes, of course! **I borrowed** it │ after breakfast.
                                            early this morning.
                                            from John.
                                            before I went to work. │

Now continue their conversation. Julia also wants to know about:

1 Ronnie's birth certificate   4 the hotel room   7 the ring
2 Ronnie's clothes   5 his bank account
3 the car   6 the champagne

What preparations do you think *Julia* has made?

51

8.2 PREPARATIONS AND RESULTS   Practice

Archibald has invited Anastasia to supper at his flat. He is expecting her to arrive any minute now . . .

The curtains are drawn.
The lights are all off except one.
There's a record on – soft music.
The table is laid for two.
The candles are lit.
There's a bottle of wine and two glasses on the table.
Archibald is wearing his velvet jacket and bow tie.
There's a bunch of red roses on the coffee table.

These are the *results* of Archibald's preparations. Say what Archibald *has done*.

At that moment the doorbell rings. It is Archibald's mother. She wants to know why Archibald has done all these things. Work in pairs.

Pair A: You are Archibald's mother, and you're very suspicious. Think what questions you will ask your son.
Pair B: You are Archibald, and you don't want your mother to know what's going on. Think what excuses you will make to her.

Now form new pairs, (one A and one B), and act out the conversation.

8.3 LEAVING NOTES   Writing

You are going away for the weekend. It is your friend's birthday, and you are letting him use your flat while you are away to give a birthday party. Before you leave, you write him a note, saying what you have done, and asking him to do things.
Work in pairs. Write the note, using these topics to help you:

cleaning	key
furniture	house plants
food	cat
drink	neighbours

Pass your note to another pair.

Write a reply to the note you have received. Imagine you have had the party. Write about:
1 what *happened* at the party
2 what you *have done* in preparation for your friend's return

You will hear a conversation between Alan and his flatmate, Charles. Listen to the
conversation and answer the questions.

1 What has Charles been doing all day? *working on his first T*
2 What three things has he done? *design the front cupboard, the list of, thought of the good title.*
3 How much has he written so far? *2 pages*
4 What hasn't he done yet? *he hasn't write design what happen next.*
5 What is the difference between the Present Perfect Continuous (have been doing)
  and the Present Perfect Simple (have done)?

Make sentences from the phrases below. Which can you use with **have done**? Which
can you use with **have been doing**? Which can you use with either?

read   take photographs
read a book   take several photographs
read two books   visit museums
do the washing-up   visit two museums and an art gallery
wash all the glasses

8.5 RECENT ACTIVITIES   Practice

Work in groups. Ask each other questions as in the example. Give as many different
explanations as you can.

Example A: Why are your eyes all red?
           B: I've been crying.
           C: I've been peeling onions.
           D: I've been watching *Love Story* on television.

Ask why:
1 your hair's wet
2 you're out of breath
3 you've got oil on your hands
4 your hands are shaking
5 your face is red
6 you've got blood on your hands
7 there's sawdust on the floor

What do you think these people   (a) have been doing recently?
                                  (b) haven't been doing recently?

1 Eric has put on six kilos.
2 Samantha has lost her suntan.
3 Michael's got severe toothache.
4 Janice isn't going to pass her exam.

Work in pairs.

Example A: You look tired. What have you been doing?
B: I've been redecorating my flat.
A: | How much have you done?
      | How far have you got with it?
B: Well, so far I've done the ceiling and I've papered the walls, but I haven't painted the woodwork yet.

Have conversations like this about:

1 cleaning the living room
2 typing letters
3 revising for the exam
4 building a house

5 making the supper
6 getting the flat ready for a party
7 organising your brother's wedding

Work in groups. Tell each other what you have really been doing recently, and what particular things you have done.

8.7   A BUSY TIME   Writing

Here is part of a letter:

I've been doing a lot of work on my flat over the past few weeks. I've taken up the dirty old lino that was there before, and sanded all the floors, except in the kitchen, where I've put cork tiles on the floor. I've also stripped off all that hideous flowery wallpaper, and yesterday I started painting the walls white. And I've been going round second-hand shops looking for cheap furniture. I haven't bought much yet, but I've got two very nice armchairs which I found in a sale a few weeks ago – I got them for £10 each.

In the same way, choose one of the sentences below, and develop it into a paragraph.

1 I've been getting my life organised recently.
2 I've been finding out about holiday jobs over the past couple of weeks.
3 I've been keeping very fit lately.
4 I've been living a wild life for the past three months.

8.8 RECENT DEVELOPMENTS   Free practice

Work in groups. Talk about:
a) what kind of things have been going on
b) what particular things have happened

in 1 your area
    2 your country
    3 the world

8.9 SUMMER JOBS   Listening ⌷

You will hear an interview with some students who are doing holiday jobs in
Brighton. Listen to the interview and answer the questions.

1 Where have the following people been working?
   a) Christine   b) Kevin   c) Kevin's brother
2 Christine has been working mostly in which part of the day?
   a) the morning
   b) the afternoon
   c) the evening
3 Which of these statements about Christine are true and which are false?
   a) The most enjoyable part of being in Brighton for her has been the job.
   b) She has had free meals and accommodation.
   c) She has made a fortune in Brighton.
   d) She hasn't spent much money.
   e) She has been working as a waitress some of the time.
   f) She finds Brighton an interesting place.
4 Kevin's been doing two different kinds of work. What are they?
5 What was Kevin's main reason for coming to Brighton?
6 Why is Kevin's brother particularly lucky?
7 Write in the missing words.

Christine: No, it hasn't been too bad. I ....,

             in fact. Not so much ...., but the people ....

             and the friends ...., and I've managed to do lots of things

             .... It's a seaside town, ...

             .... in the evenings – you know, ...

             .... and so on. And on my afternoons

             off ....

             ....

Unit 8 Summary of language

In this unit you have learnt how to:
– talk about recent past actions and their present results
– talk about recent activities and achievements

KEY POINTS

1 *Present Perfect Simple and Past Simple tenses*
   I've booked some seats for the theatre.
   I booked some seats for the theatre yesterday.

   Have you packed the picnic?
   Yes, **I have** – I packed it before breakfast.

2 *Present Perfect and Present tenses*
   I've turned off the electricity.
   The electricity **is** turned off.

   She's **put** some milk in the fridge.
   There **is** some milk in the fridge.

3 *Present Perfect Continuous and Simple*
   I've been looking for a flat.
   I've looked at five flats **so far**, but **I haven't** found one I like **yet**.

Activities

FAVOURS

You are going away for a skiing holiday for ten days during the next month. You want someone to do *five* of the things below some time during that month. Choose the things you want people to do, and write them in the table below. For each one write the exact date(s) and a reason.

lend you their car
give you a lift to the airport
lend you their ski-boots
lend you a top hat
lend you their house for a week

look after your cat while you're away
water your flowers while you're away
lend you £100
look after your children for a day
help you decorate your living room for four days

	I want someone to:	Exact date(s)	Reason
	I'm going to be on holiday from .... to .... (inclusive)		
1			
2			
3			
4			
5			

Ask other people to help you with the five things, and explain why you want them to help. They will ask you to do things too: when you agree to do something, write it in the table below.

I have agreed to:	Who for?	Exact date(s)

COMPOSITION

Write 100–150 words on one of the following topics.

1 Write a letter to a friend describing a difficult situation you are going through at the moment.
2 A friend has written asking if he/she can come and stay with you. Reply explaining that this would not be a good time.
3 Write a letter to a friend telling him/her what your plans are for the next 12 months.

SITUATIONS

1 You get on a crowded train and see one empty seat. What do you say to the person sitting in the next seat?
2 You're walking down the street with a friend when you meet another friend. They don't know each other. Introduce them to each other, giving some information about each of them, and how you first met.
3 Your grandmother is flying in from the United States this afternoon, and you want to leave work early to go and meet her. What do you say to your boss?
4 A friend says to you, 'You look worn out'. Tell him/her why.
5 Some people in front of you in the theatre are talking, and spoiling the play for you. What do you say to them?
6 A foreign friend asks you about the current fashions in clothes in your country. What do you say?
7 Your brother's about to leave for the airport. Check that he's made all necessary preparations.

Unit 9   Comparison

9.1   COMPARISON OF ADJECTIVES

Presentation

Corner shops **are friendlier than** supermarkets. Supermarkets **aren't as friendly as** corner shops.

Corner shops **are more expensive than** supermarkets. Supermarkets **aren't as expensive as** corner shops.

1   Compare corner shops and supermarkets using these adjectives:
cheap
convenient
hygienic

2   Which type of shop
   a) has a wider range of goods?
   b) gives better service?
   c) is pleasanter to shop at?
3   Which would you rather shop at?

Practice

Now compare these cars and fires in the same way. Which would you rather have?

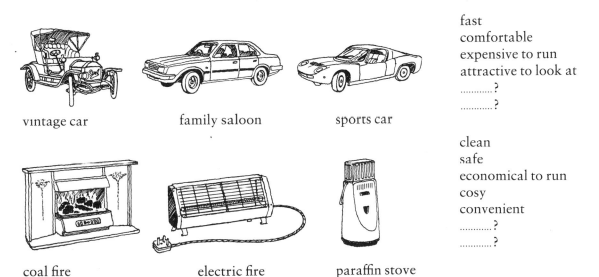

vintage car

family saloon

sports car

fast
comfortable
expensive to run
attractive to look at
............?
............?

clean
safe
economical to run
cosy
convenient
............?
............?

coal fire

electric fire

paraffin stove

Britain   Japan   India   Saudi Arabia   Turkey

Which of the five countries above is being described in each of these sentences?

1 It's richer than Britain, and it's not as industrialised as Japan.
2 It's hotter than Britain and it isn't as rich as Turkey.
3 It's much bigger than Turkey, but it's got a much smaller population.

Work in groups.
Student A: Describe one item in a set by making two comparisons.
The others: Guess which item student A is describing. The student who guesses
             correctly goes next.

1 Hong Kong   Paris   Beirut   Helsinki   Athens

2 iron   wood   plastic   glass   gold

3 carrier bag   suitcase   trunk

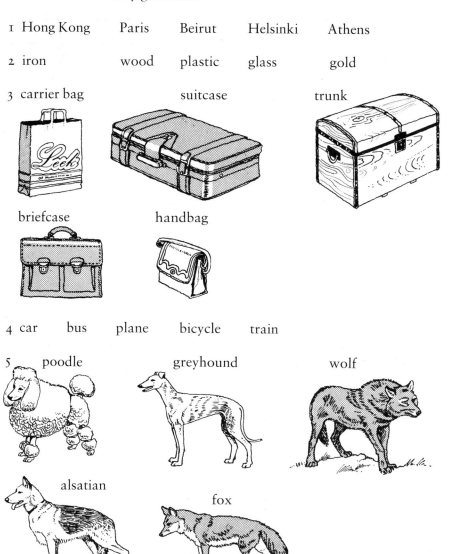

briefcase   handbag

4 car   bus   plane   bicycle   train

5   poodle   greyhound   wolf

alsatian   fox

6 Margaret Thatcher   Jackie Onassis   Ella Fitzgerald   Mrs Gandhi   Jane Fonda

7 Mick Jagger   Elton John   Paul McCartney   Frank Sinatra   Tom Jones

Look at the five countries again.
1 Which has the largest population?
2 Which is the richest country?
3 Which is the most mountainous?
4 Which is the furthest east?

Now ask similar questions about the other seven sets.

9.3 WHICH WOULD YOU RATHER?

Free practice

Would you rather . . .

. . . stay at a hotel or a bed and breakfast place?
. . . have a dog or a cat?
. . . live in a city or a village?

Work in groups. Discuss the questions above by making comparisons.

Writing

Choose one of the topics you discussed. Write a paragraph based on your discussion.

9.4 COMPARISON OF ADVERBS

Presentation

Look at these examples:

She paints **beautifully**.
She paints **more beautifully** than I do.

She writes **neatly**.
She writes **more neatly** than I do.

She works **hard**.
She works **harder** than I do.

When do we make comparative adverbs (1) with **more**? (2) with **-er**?   ⟫→

Practice

  A: He works hard, doesn't he?
  B: Oh I don't know. I work much harder than he does.
  A: Of course – nobody works as hard as you do.

Have more conversations like this. Begin with these sentences:

1 He gets up early, doesn't he?
2 She smokes heavily, doesn't she?
3 He played well, didn't he?
4 He can dance beautifully, can't he?
5 They live dangerously, don't they?
6 She can run fast, can't she?
7 They stay up late, don't they?
8 She behaved badly, didn't she?

Look at the example, and have similar conversations.

Example: *Work/fast*
        Work/quick

A: Can't you work a bit | more quickly | than that?
                        | faster |

B: No, I can't. I'm working as | quickly | as I can.
                               | fast |

1 play/quiet   5 speak/clear
2 type/careful   6 write/neat
3 drive/fast   7 stretch/far
4 dance/good   8 walk/straight

9.5 COMPARISONS INVOLVING VERBS

Presentation and practice

Complete the following sentences so that they mean the same as the sentences in italics.

1 *He earns £90 a week but he spends £100 a week.*
   a) He spends more ....
   b) He doesn't earn ....

2 *That cheese smells terrible but it tastes very good.*
   a) That cheese tastes much better ....
   b) That cheese doesn't taste ....

Now do the same with these sentences:

1 She plays the piano quite well, but she sings even better.
2 That chair is really very comfortable, though it doesn't look it.
3 He goes running every morning, and he plays squash twice a week.
4 She doesn't sound very friendly on the telephone, but she's really extremely friendly.
5 He bought three kilos of sausages, but we only needed two.

Work in groups. You are working for the state salary commission, and you have been asked to decide on fair salaries for these groups of workers:

nurses

policemen

miners

teachers

long-distance lorry drivers

Compare the five jobs, and decide who should earn the most, and who should earn the least. Consider these factors:

training   working conditions   responsibility
hours worked   job satisfaction

Tell other groups what you have decided.

Reading

Read these two advertisements, and then answer the questions.

When you stretch out in the sun you can do one of three things.

You can use no sun tan oil. You can use an ordinary sun tan oil. Or you can use Bergasol.

If you don't use any sun tan oil at all when you're in sun that is stronger than you're used to, you will burn surprisingly quickly.

If you use an ordinary sun tan oil you will protect your skin to a lesser or greater degree. How much depends on the 'protection-factor number' on the bottle.

Some of these oils block out so many of the sun's rays you can stay in the sun all day without burning—but you won't go very brown, either.

Bergasol will protect your skin like an ordinary sun tan oil. But Bergasol oil also has a tan accelerator which comes from the oil of the Bergamot fruit.

It speeds up the rate at which the sun activates the skin cells that produce melanin.

And it is melanin which gives the skin its brown colour.

So when you use Bergasol sun tan oil you go brown faster, and as the days pass the difference will become more and more obvious.

Unfortunately this special formulation isn't cheap to prepare. So Bergasol is rather more expensive than ordinary sun tan oil.

However the price looks more attractive as you do.

bergasol®

It makes you go brown faster

Protection

Many people imagine that 'cover-up' means you don't get a tan. Nothing to show for your holiday. What a shame.

Not so. With 'cover up', you can get brown if you want to. The point of cover-up is to protect your skin from the harmful rays of the sun— the ones which, according to the experts, make your skin look older.

That's what Solex Cover-up is all about—protection for your skin. It has a Sun Protection Factor of 8, which makes it suitable for anyone.

Find out how it works for you by consulting the Solex Sun Chart. On sale wherever Solex is.

With Solex Cover-up, you can tan as slowly as you like. As gently as you like. And with much less chance of peeling.

Your tan will look better. Your skin will stay young longer. Solex Cover-up.

SOLEX

Gentle tan...full protection

1 What is the main problem of someone with a sensitive skin who wants to get a suntan?

2 According to the advertisements, what is the main advantage of using:
a) Bergasol?
b) Solex?

3 What happens if you use a suntan oil with:
a) a higher protection factor number?
b) a lower protection factor number?

4 Complete the following sentences, using comparison structures.

a) If you use Bergasol, your skin cells ....

b) With Bergasol, you .... than with ordinary suntan oils.

c) Ordinary suntan oils cost ....

d) Because of the burning radiation of the sun, many people's skin

....

e) With Solex you tan .... than with Bergasol.

f) If you use Solex, your skin ....

5 Explain 'However, the price looks more attractive as you do' in the Bergasol advertisement.

Discussion

Which of the advertisements do you think is more 'scientific'?

Which would you use, Bergasol or Solex? Why?

9.8 ADVERTISEMENTS

Free practice

Work in groups. You work for an advertising agency. Choose one of the products below. What advantages do you think it might have over its competitors?

SEA-FRESH DEODORANT
CHEVROLET 8000X COUPE
SNOW-BRIGHT WASHING POWDER
THE INSTA-FLASH CAMERA
THE 'MIDGET' CASSETTE RECORDER

Writing

Write an advertisement for the product you have discussed.

Unit 9   Summary of language

In this unit you have learnt how to:
– compare advantages and disadvantages
– talk about significant differences
– compare what people do

KEY POINTS

1 *Comparison of adjectives*
Leather is strong**er than** plastic.
Plastic isn't **as** strong **as** leather.

Cars are **more** expensive to run **than** motorbikes.
Motorbikes aren't **as** expensive to run **as** cars.

2 *Comparison of adverbs*
I write **more** carefully **than** he does.
She can swim fast**er than** I can.
Can't you drive a bit **more** slowly (than that)?
They're working **as** hard **as** they can.

3 *Comparisons involving two verbs*
He sings better than he dances.
That dog isn't as dangerous as it looks.

4 *Superlative forms*
The Soviet Union is **the** largest country in the world.
She has **the most** beautiful voice (of all of us).
He smokes **the most** heavily (of all of us), but he also works **the** hardest.

5 *Vocabulary*
adjectives and adverbs

Unit 10   The past and the present

10.1   USED TO

Presentation

Many Eskimos no longer live as they used to. They live in houses, and they work in factories and for American oil companies. Many Eskimos have become completely Americanised – they wear Western clothes, they go to school, and most of them speak English. Instead of hunting and fishing, they buy food from supermarkets: they even buy frozen meat and vegetables.

Say:

1 what Eskimos │ **didn't use to do** │
   │ **used not to do** │
2 what Eskimos **used to do**

Practice

The sentences below are concerned with *habitual past actions* or with *past states*. Change them using **used to**.

1 He lived in France as a boy.
2 At one time there were trees in the garden.
3 They didn't go out in those days.
4 I was in love with her.
5 We went to school together.
6 How did you spend the winter evenings?
7 Trains were driven by steam at one time.
8 There was widespread unemployment at that time.
9 What did you do in the summer in those days?
10 We had our milk delivered.

Practice

Work in groups. From the information in the pictures, talk about what life used to be like in Victorian times. Use **used to** and the Past Simple tense.

Writing

Now write a paragraph based on the pictures. Add any details you like.

10.3 REMEMBERING THE PAST

Presentation

You will hear someone talking about how she used to spend her time as a child.
Listen to the tape and answer the questions.

1 What does the speaker say about:
   a) the pond by her grandfather's sawmill?
   b) the apple trees?
   c) her bike?
   d) her mother?

2 Exactly what does she say using:
   a) **I remember**?
   b) **used to**?
   c) **would**?

Free practice

Work in groups. Tell the others about when you were a child. Talk about:

1 what you used to do
2 what other members of your family used to do

Here are some ideas:

playing	birthdays	visits
punishments	Christmas	early schooldays

10.4 THINGS HAVE CHANGED   Presentation and practice

You're talking to a friend you haven't seen for some time. Have conversations as in
the example.

Example A: How's Newcastle?

B: Oh, **I don't** live in Newcastle **any** | more.
                                            | longer.

A: Oh, you've moved, have you?
B: Yes, I bought a cottage in Wales a few months ago. It's quite nice,
   actually ...

1 How are you getting on at college?
2 How are you and Pat getting on?
3 How's the dog?
4 Still having trouble with that old car of yours?
5 How are Fred and Janet?
6 Have you got a cigarette?
7 How about a game of tennis?
8 Pauline's still in hospital, I suppose?

Now write sentences, explaining each change.
Example Florence doesn't live in Newcastle any longer; she's moved to Wales.

10.5 THE PRESENT PERFECT PASSIVE

Presentation

Belcombe used to be an unspoilt village on the south coast of England, but you wouldn't recognise it now. They've developed it as a tourist resort – and they've completely destroyed its old atmosphere. They've pulled down the picturesque old cottages by the harbour, and they've built a hideous luxury hotel there instead. They've widened and resurfaced all the old cobbled streets, and they've cut down the trees in the village square, and put a car park there. Even the old village shop isn't there any more – they've turned it into one of those awful cafés where everything seems to be made of plastic, and they've put a big sign outside saying 'Ye Olde Tea Shoppe'.

The passage tells you *what they have done* to the village. Instead, we could talk about *what has happened* to the village.

Example They've developed the village as a tourist resort.
The village **has been developed** as a tourist resort.

Use the Passive to talk about the other changes in the village.

1 The atmosphere of the village . . .
2 The old cottages . . .
3 A luxury hotel . . .
4 The streets . . .
5 The trees in the square . . .
6 A car park . . .
7 The village shop . . .
8 A sign saying 'Ye Olde Tea Shoppe' . . .

Practice

The two pictures below show how a street has changed.

Work in pairs. Ask each other what has happened to everything. Answer using the Passive.

Example A: What's happened to the shop?
             B: It's been pulled down and a garage has been built there instead.

10.6 CHANGES OF HABIT   Practice

Work in pairs. Interview each other about how much/how often you do the things
below compared to a few years ago. Make a note of your partner's answers.

Example A: Do you go to parties as often as you used to?
          B: Yes – I go to parties more often now than I used to.
          or No – I don't go to parties as often as I used to.
          or Well, I don't go to parties any more.

		more/less
1	go to parties (often)	1
2	cinema (often)	2
3	cry (often)	3
4	smoke (much)	4
5	eat (much)	5
6	travel (much)	6
7	read (much)	7
8	write letters (often)	8
9	lose your temper (often)	9

Now use your notes to tell someone else how your partner has changed.

Example He doesn't go to parties as often as he used to.

Work in groups. Tell the others some other ways in which you've changed over the
past few years.

10.7 MODERN DEVELOPMENTS

Free practice

Work in groups. Discuss how these modern developments have changed people's
everyday lives. For each one, talk about:
1 what things used to be like
2 what things are like now
3 how things have changed

television	cassette tapes
pocket calculators	supersonic airliners
the telephone	convenience foods

Writing

Choose one of the developments you discussed. Write a short article (100–150 words)
saying what good and bad effects it has had.

10.8 HALLOWE'EN

Reading

Read the passage and answer the questions that follow it.

Hallowe'en is the last night of October, and it used to be thought the most enchanted night of the year. It was the night when witches and evil spirits came back on earth to weave their magic spells. Superstitious people kept up many strange old customs in an effort to keep these evil influences away. Farmers used to light big fires in their fields, and the farm workers and their families would walk around the fields singing old songs and hymns. At intervals, the strange procession would stop to hear the local priest offer prayers to the good spirits, and ask them to help keep the evil ones away.

Great care was taken that none of the farm animals were left in the fields. They would all be locked up safely in their stables and sheds, and over each of the stable and shed doors a few rowan leaves would be hung. Witches and evil spirits would not go anywhere near the rowan tree.

In more recent times, Hallowe'en has become a time for parties, when children dress up as witches and play all kinds of special games such as 'ducking for the apple'. After the games there is often a big supper with plenty of pumpkin pie, cakes and a lot of other delicious things to eat.

But for the most part the children enjoy the fun of dressing up and playing their favourite game of 'Trick or Treat'. They run down each street knocking on the doors crying loudly 'Trick or Treat!', and most people have some sweets ready to give them. Those that do not can expect maybe to have a tyre flattened, or their windows covered in soap. Or the children may just knock on the door and run away.

Many of the houses have a jack-o'-lantern in their windows, which are hollowed out pumpkins with candles burning inside them. But in this modern age many of the pumpkins are being replaced with plastic electric ones that can be brought out each year.

1 In one sentence, say:
  a) why people used to think Hallowe'en was important
  b) why people celebrate it nowadays

2 Make a list of *six* old customs that we would call 'superstitious'.

3 a) How do you think the game 'Ducking for the apple' might be played?
  b) Why is the game 'Trick or Treat' so called?

4 Does Hallowe'en exist in your own country? If so, how is it different? If not, what is the most similar festival?

Writing

1 Write down a list of *five* things that children do on Hallowe'en.
2 Imagine you were one of these children, but have now grown up. You are telling a friend what you *used to do* on Hallowe'en when you were young. Write your description of what you used to do.

Unit 10   Summary of language

In this unit you have learnt how to:
– talk about past habits and states
– remember the past
– talk about recent changes
– compare the past and the present

KEY POINTS

1 *'Used to'*
We **used to** live in Wales.
I **used to be** driven to school in the morning.

People | **used not to** / **didn't use to** | travel abroad much.

Where **did** you **use to** go for your holidays?

2 *Other structures for remembering the past*
I **remember** play**ing** in the park when I was young.
I **remember** we used to fish in the canal, but we **would** never catch anything.

3 *'Not . . . any more/longer'*

We **don't** go out together **any** | **more.** / **longer.** | (We've stopped going out together.)

He **hasn't** got his car **any** | **more.** / **longer.** | (He's sold it.)

4 *Present Perfect Passive*
They've pulled the hotel down.
The hotel **has been pulled** down.

They've turned the old houses into offices.
The old houses **have been turned** into offices.

5 *Time comparison*
I don't go to the theatre **as** often **as I used to.**
I **used to** go to the theatre **more** often **than I do now.**

I laugh **more** than I **used to.**
I **used to** laugh **less than I do now.**

Activities

BALLOON DEBATE

Four famous people are in a balloon over the
Atlantic, and the balloon is slowly dropping
towards the sea. It can only carry one person
safely: three of the balloonists are going to
have to jump out of the balloon, so that one
can survive. Each of the four people on
board thinks that he or she should be the
one to stay on board . . .

Students A, B, C and D: You are the four
people in the balloon. Decide who you
are (you can be *any* famous person,
alive or dead), and prepare a two-minute
speech, saying why you should be the
one to be saved. In your speech say:
a) what you have achieved in your life
b) what you intend to achieve in the
future
c) why your life is more important than
the others.

PROCEDURE

1 In turn, the four balloonists give their
speeches to the class.
2 The class can ask any of the balloonists
any questions they like.
3 The balloonists give a short closing speech,
summarising their arguments.
4 The class votes. The balloonist who stays
in the balloon is the winner.

COMPOSITION

Who do you think is *either* the greatest living musician *or* the greatest living writer *or*
the greatest living statesman?

Write 100–150 words saying why you have chosen him/her.

Unit 11 Likes and dislikes

11.1 DEGREES OF ENJOYMENT   Presentation

2./

know what I'm going to do with them – they're so completely different.
Alice loves sunbathing all day, and Sidney loathes "sitting around
on crowded beaches doing nothing". He's fond of tennis, and enjoys
walking – Alice (as you can imagine!) doesn't like any kind of sport.
She's not very fond of cooking, either. Well I don't mind cooking, but
Sidney adores garlic – he won't eat a meal without it. Alice (of
course!) hates eating anything with garlic in it, and I don't like
it much myself, so you can imagine the arguments we have at
mealtimes.

   And then the evenings. Alice is crazy about dancing, so we have to
go to the disco every night. I don't mind discos myself but it's
obvious that Sidney can't stand them. He just sits there looking
miserable. He'd much rather be having a quiet beer in the pub
– and so would I, to be honest. Alice, of course, wouldn't be
seen dead in a pub – she says they're boring! I just can't see why
they go on holiday together. The only thing they both seem to
enjoy is watching old films on the television; and, as you know
I hate wasting my time in front of the T.V. Still, at least it
stops them arguing.
         Help!!!
            all my love
               Cilla

Complete the table below to show how much Alice, Sidney and Cilla like the
activities mentioned in the letter.

	No!	*No*	*—*	*Yes*	*Yes!*
Alice					sunbathing
Sidney	sitting on beaches			tennis	
Cilla			going to discos		

Now use the information in the table to talk about how much Alice, Sidney and Cilla
enjoy each activity.

77

11.2 RESPONDING TO SUGGESTIONS   Practice

Work in pairs. Find out how much your partner likes doing the things below, by making *particular suggestions*, as in the examples. Choose activities in any order you like.

Examples: *flying*
          A: Would you like to come to the States with me?
          B: No thanks – I can't stand flying.

          watching horror films
          A: Let's go and see *Son of Frankenstein.*
          B: That's a good idea – I love watching horror films.

sitting in the sun   eating spicy food
skiing   learning languages
dancing   getting up early
looking after children   cooking
sitting in crowded places   going for long walks
dressing up   talking to foreigners

11.3 PREFERENCES

Presentation

You will hear someone being asked if he prefers driving or being a passenger. Listen to the tape and answer the questions.

1 What is the woman's first question?
2 a) When does the man enjoy driving?
  b) When doesn't he enjoy driving?
3 What does he feel about being a passenger?
4 Complete this sentence:
  On the whole he prefers .... to ....

  because ....

Practice

Work in pairs. Interview each other in the same way. Ask about the following topics:

1 driving/being a passenger
2 swimming in a pool/swimming in the sea
3 sharing a flat/living alone
4 working outside/working inside

After each interview write a sentence explaining what your partner prefers, and why.

11.4 YOUR OWN LIKES AND DISLIKES   Free practice

Work in groups. Find out from each other what you really like and dislike doing.
Talk about your *favourite* activities, and also things you *particularly* dislike.
Ask about:

travel	in the summer	in class
eating out	clothes	when you're alone
parties	when it's raining	

11.5 THINGS THAT HAPPEN TO YOU

Presentation

'... Well, I just love people asking me for my
autograph, though I don't like being pushed about by
crowds of fans at airports ... Of course I hate having
my films criticised in the newspapers ... No I don't
mind being told what to do by the director – that's
his job, isn't it? But I don't like being ordered about
by camera crews, or people like that ... Oh yes, I
love having my work praised, and I adore people
telling me what a wonderful actress I am. Basically, I
suppose I just love being loved ...'

The sentences below show some of the film star's other likes and dislikes. Change
them using either **being** or **having**.

1 I hate people telephoning me early in
   the morning.
2 I love people taking my photograph.
3 I like people admiring my clothes.

4 I don't mind journalists following me about.
5 I enjoy people taking me to expensive restaurants.
6 I love people bringing my breakfast to me in bed.
7 I adore people giving me expensive presents.

Practice

Examples A: How do you feel if someone tickles you?
            B: I hate **people tickling** me.
            C: Really? I don't mind **being tickled**.

            A: How do you feel if someone admires your clothes?
            B: I love **people admiring** my clothes.
            C: Yes, I like **having** my clothes **admired** too.

Work in threes. Have similar conversations. How do you feel if someone:

1 interrupts you?
2 twists your arm?
3 compliments you?
4 tells you what to do?
5 takes your temperature?
6 laughs at you?
7 corrects your English?
8 scratches your back?

11.6 TYPES OF PEOPLE

Free practice

Work in groups.
What do you think the following people like/don't mind/don't like about (a) the things they do? (b) the things that happen to them?

1 a football star
2 a beggar
3 a journalist
4 a small child

Writing

Imagine that you are one of the four people. Write a paragraph about your likes and dislikes.

11.7 PREFERRED LIFE STYLES: LIKE TO

Presentation and practice

Add a general statement, saying what each of the following people **like to do**, as in the example.

Example: Fred reads two newspapers, and watches all the current affairs
programmes on TV ...
In other words, Fred **likes to** keep up with world events.

1 Janet goes running every morning, and plays a lot of tennis. In other words, ...
2 Paul goes out every night, and has a party most weekends.
3 When she's abroad, Nora writes a lot of letters, and phones home every week.
4 Steve doesn't allow talking in class, and his students have to stand up when he comes in.
5 The Browns hoover all the carpets once a week, and dust the furniture every morning.

Continue the following:

'I like to keep busy on Sundays. I like to get up early and have a good breakfast. Then I like to write a few letters, and, if there's time, I like to do all my washing. I like to go for a walk before lunch. Then, after a light lunch, I ....
In the evening ....

Work in groups. What do you like to do:
1 when you wake up?
2 the day before a big exam?
3 before you go away on holiday?

Writing

Choose two of these sentences, and develop them into paragraphs. Use **like to** and the Present Simple.

1 I like to be independent . . .
2 I like to keep a record of everything I do . . .
3 I like to get the most out of my visits to London . . .
4 I like to look smart . . .
5 I like to keep myself to myself . . .

11.8 FOND OF FLYING

Listening

You will hear a journalist talking about flying. Listen to the whole passage, and then answer the questions.

Listen to section 1 again.
1 Do you think the journalist travels a lot?
2 What does she particularly like about flying?
3 According to the journalist what do other people say about flying?
4 What doesn't she like doing? Why?

Listen to section 2 again.
5 Which does she prefer – long flights or short flights? Why?
6 In general, there are *three* things she dislikes about very long flights. What are they?
7 What does she like to do on very long flights?
8 Why do the cabin staff wake passengers up?

Writing

Develop your answers to questions 1–8 into two paragraphs, summarising what the journalist says about flying.

Discussion

1 What do you like and dislike about flying?
2 For long journeys, do you prefer travelling by bus, train or car? Why?

Unit 11   Summary of language

In this unit you have learnt how to:
– say what you like or dislike doing, and how much
– say what you like or dislike other people doing to you
– state your preferences
– talk about your preferred life-style

KEY POINTS

1 *Active and passive gerund forms*
I enjoy swimm**ing**.
I'm fond of go**ing** to the opera.

I love **people** invit**ing** me to parties.
I love **being** invited to parties.

She doesn't like **people** pull**ing** her hair.
She doesn't like **having** her hair pull**ed**.

2 *'Prefer'*
Which do you prefer, eat**ing** at home **or** eat**ing** in restaurants?
I prefer eat**ing** in restaurants.
I prefer eat**ing** in restaurants **to** eat**ing** at home.

3 *'Like doing' and 'like to do'*
I like eat**ing** caviare.
I like **to** have a good breakfast in the morning.

4 *Vocabulary*
'like' and 'dislike' verbs

Unit 12 Events and circumstances

12.1 EVENTS AND CIRCUMSTANCES

Presentation

Read the four passages below, and answer the questions.

A I first met your father while we were living in London, about 20 years ago. I was having lunch in a small café in Kensington when he walked in and asked if he could share my table . . .

B Poor Mrs Phillips. She was walking down the High Street yesterday when a chimney fell off one of the houses and crashed onto the pavement. It missed her by inches . . .

C The tiles were uncovered accidentally by workmen while they were laying a gas main. An expert from the museum was called in, and he identified them as part of a Roman villa . . .

D I remember it as if it was yesterday. We were all sitting in the kitchen playing cards when the music suddenly stopped and they announced that he was dead. We just couldn't believe it . . .

1 a) What are the *events* in each passage?
   b) In what *circumstances* did these events occur?
2 How are (a) **when** (b) **while** used to link events and circumstances?

Practice

Match the events and circumstances in the two lists below. Join each pair using (a) **when** (b) **while** as in the example.

Example He was painting the ceiling **when** he fell off the ladder.
           He fell off the ladder **while** he was painting the ceiling.

Events	*Circumstances*
He fell off the ladder.	He was writing a cheque.
His jeans split.	He was tidying his room.
He burnt his hand.	He was climbing over the fence.
The TV screen went blank.	He was having breakfast.
He lost consciousness.	He was painting the ceiling.
The tyre burst.	He was taking the meat out of the oven.
He found his passport.	He was being given the injection.
His pen ran out.	He was turning a corner.
He bit his tongue.	He was watching the news.

> A: I saw an accident yesterday.
> B: What were you doing at the time?
> A: I was queueing for the cinema.
> C: And what did you do when you saw the accident?
> A: I rushed forward to see if I could help.

Work in threes. Have similar conversations, beginning with these remarks:

1 I broke a tooth this morning.
2 I got cramp in my leg yesterday afternoon.
3 The au pair girl broke two glasses yesterday.
4 We were chased by a bull last week.
5 Jack cut his face this morning.
6 She lost the top of her bikini yesterday afternoon.

Report your answers to the rest of the class.

Example I was queueing for the cinema yesterday when I saw a car accident, so I
rushed forward to see if I could help.

12.3 HEADLINE NEWS

Practice

Look at the newspaper headlines below, and explain what they mean.

Example

Express derailed at 90 mph

An express train was derailed while it was travelling at 90 miles per hour.

Boeing 747 hijacked over Atlantic
150 arrested in anti-nuclear demonstration
Ambassador's son kidnapped on way to school
Tomatoes thrown at Minister during speech
Man with bomb arrested at Heathrow
GOLFER STRUCK BY LIGHTNING

Writing

Choose one of the headlines and develop it into a paragraph. Add any details you
like, and add at least one more event.

Example An express train was travelling at 90 m.p.h. on the main line from London
to Manchester last night when it was derailed by a tree which was lying on
the line. Fortunately, no-one was killed, although 30 passengers were taken
to hospital suffering from minor injuries.

12.4 EXPERIENCES

Free practice

You will hear two people talking about experiences they have had. Listen to the tape and answer the questions.

1 What is the man's story?
2 What is the woman's story?

Work in groups. Have similar conversations, talking about experiences that you have had. Begin by asking each other these questions:

1 Have you ever been chased by a dog?   3 Have you ever been stopped by a policeman?
2 Have you ever lost all your money?   4 Have you ever been in a dangerous situation?

Writing

Choose one of the stories that you told or heard. Write a paragraph telling the story of what happened.

12.5 EVIDENCE OF THE SENSES   Presentation

Look at these examples.

A   Through my binoculars I could see the girl across the street sunbathing on her balcony. But she noticed me looking at her. Then I saw her blush, pick up her magazine, and go indoors.

B   Last night as I was going to bed I could hear the neighbours shouting and throwing crockery at each other. Then, a few moments later, I heard a door slam, and everything went quiet.

C   'Now you say someone took your wallet out of the back pocket of your trousers while you were standing in the bus queue. Are you sure it didn't just fall out?'
'No, I'm quite sure – I actually felt someone take it out of my pocket.'
'And when you turned round, there was a young man running away down the street. Is that correct?'
'Yes, I saw him running away.'
'And did anyone else see all this happen?'

What is the difference between:
see/hear/feel someone **do** something
and
see/hear/feel someone **doing** something?

Put the verbs in brackets into the correct form.
1 I could see a man (sit) on the balcony and (read) a newspaper. Then I saw him (get) up and (go) indoors.
2 I turned round and saw a snake slowly (slither) towards me.

85

3 I could hear a car (come) fast along the main road. I heard the driver (brake) hard.
4 I thought I heard someone (break) a window in the next room.
5 I heard the bomb (explode), and felt the whole building (shake).
6 I heard them (talk) in a low voice, and then suddenly I heard someone (shout) 'Help!'

12.6 WITNESSES   Practice

Work in pairs. You are pair A or pair B.

Pair A
You live opposite a house where a murder was committed.

1 Read the story of what you saw and heard.
2 With your partner, practise retelling it, using wherever possible:
I saw/heard
I could see/hear

I was standing on my balcony on the first floor. Some children were playing in the street. Then a car came down the road, and stopped on the other side, just opposite my house. There were two men in the car. One got out. He said to the other, 'This won't take long.' He rang the doorbell of the house opposite. Mrs Jones opened the door and the man went inside. A few minutes later there was a shot from inside the house. Immediately after that, the door opened suddenly and the man came running out. He got into the car, and they drove away. Someone in the house opposite was screaming.

Pair B
You were a tenant in a house where a murder was committed.

1 Read the story of what you saw and heard.
2 With your partner, practise retelling it, using wherever possible:
I saw/heard/felt/smelt
I could see/hear/feel/smell

It was breakfast time. I was getting dressed. There was bacon frying downstairs in the kitchen, and Mrs Jones was hoovering the hall. The doorbell rang. Mrs Jones stopped the hoover and opened the door. She was talking to the man. Then she shouted to her husband, 'It's for you.' There was a pause. I went to listen from the top of the stairs: now the two men were exchanging angry words in a foreign language. Then somebody fired a shot. The whole house shook. Mrs Jones screamed. A cold sweat began to run down my back. I went downstairs. Mr Jones was lying motionless on the floor. There was blood coming from a wound in his chest.

Form new pairs (one A and one B). Compare in as much detail as you can what you both saw, heard, etc.

12.7 RUPERT AND THE SPACE PIRATES   Writing

1 Look at the four pairs of pictures, which give the outline of a science fiction story.

2 Decide what happened.

3 Write the story. Begin:
'One evening, Rupert was sitting on his porch admiring the night sky when . . .'

Next Day...

That Night...

Next Evening...

12.8 THE GHOST OF FERNIE CASTLE

Listening 📼

You will hear someone describing an experience she had at a hotel in Scotland. Listen to the tape and answer the questions.

1 a) What exactly did the speaker hear?
   b) What was she doing when she heard it?
   c) What did she do when she heard it?

2 How did she explain it to herself
   a) the first time?
   b) the second time?

3 How did she feel
   a) immediately afterwards?
   b) the next day?

4 a) Write down all the events that took place on the second night.
   b) Why was the speaker 'very worried'?

5 Listen to the story told by the owner of the hotel and write in the missing words.

She's supposed to be _the wife of a man_

to get married, and her father _didn't want her to marry this man_,

and they _escaped_ Fernie Castle and _hid in tiny room at the top of_

the West Tower, and her father's men _eventually tracked them down_

and _found this room_ where they _were hiding_, and there was

a terrible struggle, and somehow while she _was trying to escape_

she _fell out of the window_ and _fell three floors to her_

dead on the stone courtyard below.

6 a) In what ways does the speaker's experience fit the owner's description of the woman?
   b) The owner suggests two possible explanations for what happened. What are they?

Discussion

Work in groups.
1 Discuss what *you* think the speaker really experienced, and why.
2 Tell the others about a mysterious or 'supernatural' experience that you have had, or that you've heard about from someone else.

Unit 12 Summary of language

In this unit you have learnt how to:
– relate past events to their circumstances
– talk about the consequences of past events
– talk about what you saw, heard and felt

KEY POINTS

1 *Past Simple and Past Continuous*
He was ski**ing when** he twist**ed** his ankle.
He twist**ed** his ankle **while** he **was** skiing.

They **were** walk**ing** in the mountains **when** the mist **came** down.
The mist **came** down **while** they **were** walk**ing** in the mountains.

When the mist **came** down, they stay**ed** where they were and wait**ed** for it to clear.

2 *Present Perfect and Past tenses*
'**Have** you ever **seen** a flying saucer?'
'Yes, **I have. I saw** one last summer. **I was** walk**ing** in the mountains when I suddenly **saw** a silver object in the sky . . .'

3 *Verbs of perception + infinitive/ + -ing*
I saw the girl **faint.**
I could see smoke ris**ing** from the roof.
I heard someone **say** 'Who's there?'
I felt a bee crawl**ing** slowly up my back.

Activities

FOR BETTER, FOR WORSE

You have read a newspaper article saying how much worse life is now than it was 50 years ago. The article claims that these things in particular have changed for the worse:

relationships between people   the level of culture
attitudes of young people   the standard of education
the environment   conditions for old people

Pair A: You completely agree with the article's point of view: you think that life was much better 50 years ago than it is now. You are going to meet a friend, who you know will disagree with you. Think what you will say to him/her.

Pair B: You completely disagree with the article's point of view: you think that life is much better now than it was 50 years ago. You are going to meet a friend, who you know has the same opinions as the writer. Think what you will say to him/her.

Now form new pairs (one A and one B) and discuss what you have read.

COMPOSITION

You are a journalist. Write part of a newspaper article (100–150 words) entitled 'The last 50 years: has the quality of life improved?' Write about any of the topics you discussed.

SITUATIONS

1 You're in a restaurant. A waiter comes and takes your order. A few minutes later another waiter comes and asks you what you would like. What do you reply?
2 You've got a nasty cut on your leg. A friend sees it and asks 'How did it happen?' Tell him.
3 A foreign friend says she's going to stay at the Crown Hotel, the most expensive place in town. You don't want her to waste her money. Suggest an alternative place to stay.
4 A friend can't decide what kind of car to buy. Recommend one, and say why.
5 You've just arrived in England, and you have no English money. You need 10p for an urgent phone call. Ask a passer-by.
6 A friend suggests going to see *The Sound of Music* at the cinema. Refuse, giving a reason.
7 You've just moved into a new flat. The telephone rings, and the caller asks for Mrs Olivia, the previous owner of the flat. What do you say?

Unit 13　Leisure activities and skills

13.1　LEISURE ACTIVITIES: ADVERBS

Presentation

1 What leisure activities are shown in the pictures above?
2 Which of the activities can you talk about using **go ... ing**?

Practice

Work in groups. Find out how much the other people do each activity.

Examples　Do you listen to the radio **at all**?　　Do you go dancing **at all**?

　　　　　I listen to the radio (**quite**) **a lot**.　　I go dancing (**quite**) **a lot**.
　　　　　I **don't** listen to the radio (**very**) **much**.　　I **don't** go dancing (**very**) **much**.
　　　　　I **don't** listen to the radio (**at all**).　　I **don't** go dancing (**at all**).

13.2 THINGS YOU CAN 'DO'   Presentation and practice

I do (quite) a lot of skiing.
I don't do much skiing.
I don't do any skiing.

Talk about the following leisure activities in the same way.

fishing	walking	painting	mountain climbing
gardening	reading	photography	water-skiing
cooking	pottery	riding	dressmaking
sailing	swimming	yoga	jogging

Answer these questions in as many different ways as you can.
1 Do you swim at all?
2 Do you do any yoga?
3 Do you do much reading?

13.3 HOW MUCH?   Practice

You will hear two people playing a game.
Listen to the tape, and say how much the second person does of the following:
1 skiing
2 tennis
3 gardening

In *your own* table, write nine activities from the pictures in 13.1 and the list in 13.2, three in each column.

Work in pairs. Find out what your partner has written by asking questions.
When he/she answers 'Yes', write the activity in *his/her* table, in the correct column.

	A lot	Quite a lot	Not much
You	1 .... 2 .... 3	1 .... 2 .... 3	1 .... 2 .... 3 ....

	A lot	Quite a lot	Not much
Your Partner	1 .... 2 .... 3	1 .... 2 .... 3	1 .... 2 .... 3 ....

You will hear a description of how someone spends his free time. Listen to the tape and answer the questions.

1 What kind of person is the man?
2 Where does he spend most of his time, and doing what?
3 What does the speaker say about:
   a) the pub?   b) singing?   c) the local choir?
4 Why don't you ever see the man at weekends?

Work in groups.

1 Look at the people in the pictures. Imagine what different things they do in their spare time.
2 Choose one of the people. Write a paragraph describing how the person you have chosen spends his/her spare time.

1

2

3

4

5

13.5 SKILLS   Presentation

Read the passage below, and answer the questions.

'Of course,' he continued, taking another mouthful of steak, 'I've always been good at sports. I'm a brilliant footballer, you know – in fact, I'd say I was very good at ball games in general. I'm not bad at skiing, either. The funny thing is, my brother's completely different. He . . . I say, I'm not boring you, am I?'

She covered the yawn with her hand. 'Oh no,' she managed to say, 'I'm fascinated. Do go on.'

'Yes, well, my brother . . .' he washed the steak down with some Perrier water, 'he was always hopeless at football . . . and he's a useless skier. Not very good at tennis, either. But he's terrific at chess. Very good at using his brain, you know. Of course, I don't know one end of a chess board from the other. I think I take after my father – he's a fantastic footballer, you know, and he's quite a good tennis player, too. But then he's not bad at chess, either . . .' He stopped, obviously puzzled that his father was good at doing so many things. She was silent.

'Well,' he said at last, 'that's enough about me. Tell me – what are you good at?'

She smiled. 'Well,' she said. 'People tell me that I'm a very good listener . . .'

Complete the table below to show how good the man, his brother and his father are at the activities mentioned in the passage.

	Very good	Good	Quite good	Not very good	Very bad
The man	football				
His brother					
His father					

Now use the information in the table to talk about how good the three people are at each activity. Make *two* types of sentence for each answer, where you can.

Example   He's **brilliant at (playing) football**.
            He's **a brilliant footballer**.

13.6 ASKING FAVOURS   Practice

Example: *You have been invited to a fancy dress party.*
    A: Are you any good at dressmaking?
    B: Not bad. Why?
    A: I want someone to make me a Dracula costume.
    B: Oh. Then you want to ask Ann. She's fantastic at dressmaking.

Work in groups. Have similar conversations, asking the others to help you in different ways. You:
1 have just moved into a new house
2 have got some people coming to dinner
3 are organising a variety show for charity
4 are starting up a small business

13.7 JOBS

Practice

What different things do these people have to be good at?

a barman in a nightclub
an astronaut
an au pair girl
a spy
a teacher

Could you do these jobs? Why/Why not?

Writing

Imagine that you are applying for one of these jobs.
Write a short letter of application, including information about what you are good at.

13.8 YOUR OWN LEISURE ACTIVITIES AND SKILLS

Free practice

Work in pairs.
Find out as much as you can about your partner's leisure activities.
Find out *how much* he/she does of each activity, and *how good* he/she is at it. Ask about:

sports   reading
hobbies   other activities
social life

Write the information down in the form of notes.

Writing

Using your notes, write a paragraph about how your partner spends his/her spare time.

Reading

Read the newspaper article below, and answer the questions.

Chips with everything

'How's the basketball coming on?'

I put down my drink and looked across at the next table. Both the man and the woman were at least 65. I was curious— pensioners, as far as I know, don't play a lot of basketball.

'Oh, I'm not playing much basketball these days,' the woman replied. 'But I'm getting much better at golf—I did a round in two under par last night.'

Last night? What's this, I thought—a floodlit golf course? I opened my packet of crisps, thoughtfully. 'I'm still pretty hopeless at chess, I'm afraid,' the man said. 'It beat me on level one this morning.'

The penny dropped. These two were obviously the proud owners of video games.

It's very likely that one of the consequences of the development of the silicon chip will be that a lot of people will have a lot more leisure time. It's equally likely that the chip will have a dramatic effect on how we spend that leisure time. It already has. Space invader machines are now a familiar sight in pubs, coffee bars, take-away restaurants – even police stations. A lot of people play them, and some, particularly schoolchildren, get remarkably high scores. How, one wonders, do they find the time (and money) to become so good?

If you have your own home video set, the possibilities are endless. You can play football, tennis, golf, basketball, tenpin bowling and other active sports without stepping out of your living room. Without even moving.

You can become an expert at chess or backgammon without ever playing another human being. Indeed, human beings aren't needed at all: there is already an annual computer chess championship—computer against computer.

So, what of the future? Will we see gangs of schoolchildren robbing old ladies for the money

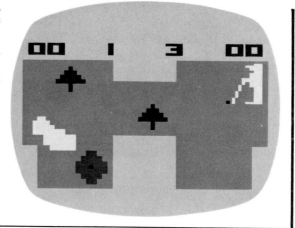

to feed space invader machines? Will football grounds lie empty as families sit at home round the TV playing video football, or watching the national video football championship? Perhaps it won't go that far. But we won't have to wait long for the Video Olympics, I'm sure of that.

Back in the pub, I stood up, took out 20 pence, and went over to the space invader machine. I may not be much good at beating computers at backgammon, but any space invaders who arrive on Earth anywhere near me had better watch out. That is, as long as they play by the rules, and fly backwards and forwards in six rows of six while I shoot them down.

1 Where is the writer at the beginning of the passage?
2 Who asks the question 'How's the basketball coming on?'
3 The people are talking about video games. How does the writer know this? Give *three* answers.
4 Explain 'The penny dropped'.
5 The writer mentions two important effects that the silicon chip will have on people's lives. What are they?
6 Two things puzzle the writer about schoolchildren and space invader machines. What are they?
7 What two types of game can you play on a home video set?
8 What effects does the writer think that video games may have on people?
9 How good is the writer at: a) playing backgammon?   b) playing space invader machines?
10 On the whole, do you think the writer approves of video games, or not?

Discussion

1 Do you play any video games? How good are you at them?
2 Do you think that (a) video games in public places (b) home video games are a good thing? What are their good and bad effects?
3 Gambling in public places is controlled by law. Do you think that video games in public places should be controlled by law as well? Why/Why not?

Unit 13   Summary of language

In this unit you have learnt how to:
– talk and ask about leisure activities
– say how much you do of a particular activity
– talk and ask about skill

KEY POINTS

1 *Questions about activities*

Do you | fish / go fishing | (at all)?
Do you play chess (at all)?
Do you do any gardening?

2 *Expressions of quantity*
I ski **quite a lot.**
I don't go swimming **very much.**
I don't play chess **at all.**

I do **a lot of** painting.
I don't do **much** waterskiing.
I don't do **any** cooking.

3 *'Skill' expressions*
Are you **any good at** dancing?
She's **terrific at** swimming.
I'm **not very good at** (playing) chess.

Are you **a good** dancer?
She's **a fantastic** swimmer.
I'm **quite a good** chess player.

4 *Vocabulary*
sports and hobbies

Unit 14   Advice

14.1   SUGGESTIONS AND ADVICE

Presentation

Alice got engaged to Don just before she went abroad on holiday, and he gave her a very expensive diamond engagement ring. When she gets back from her holiday, she realises that she's lost the ring.
Advise her what to do.

Practice

Work in groups. Advise these people what to do:
1   Jill's husband took the dog for a walk five hours ago. The dog has just come back without him.
2   Alistair has been working 12 hours a day for the last month, and he's beginning to look ill. This morning, for no reason at all, he lost his temper and shouted at everyone in the office.
3   Robin is digging in his garden when he discovers an old chest full of gold coins.

Now tell other people in the class what advice you gave.

Examples   **I advised** Alice **to** look through her handbag.
       I advised her **not to** tell Don.

   I suggested that she | should buy | another ring.
                           | bought |

14.2 ALTERNATIVE SOLUTIONS   Practice

    A: My car won't start.
    B: **Have you tried pushing** it?
    A: Yes, I've tried that, but it didn't help.
    B: Well, **why don't you try cleaning** the plugs?
    A: Oh, there's nothing wrong with the plugs – they're new.
    B: ....

Have conversations like this. Suggest as many things as you can.

1 I don't seem to be able to lose weight.
2 I've had hiccups for the last half hour.
3 I can't get to sleep at night.
4 I can't unscrew the lid of this pot of jam.
5 I'm madly in love with Michelle, but she won't even look at me.

14.3 PROBLEMS   Free practice

You will hear someone talking about a problem that she has.
Listen to the tape and answer the questions.
1 What is her problem?
2 What would you advise her to do?

Work in groups. Together, think of a problem of your own.

Form new groups. Tell your problem to other people in the group. They will advise you what to do.

14.4 TAKING PRECAUTIONS   Presentation and practice

Why is it a good idea to carry an umbrella when you go out in Britain?

> Because it **might** rain.
>
> Because | **if you don't** / **otherwise** | you **might** get wet.

Work in groups. Discuss why it is a good idea to do these other things. Say:
a) what might happen (anyway)   b) what might happen otherwise

Why is it a good idea to:
1 book seats for the theatre in advance?
2 go to the dentist regularly?
3 put a padlock on your bicycle?
4 drive slowly in very cold weather?
5 dry your hands before you do electrical repairs?
6 wear a crash helmet when you ride a motorbike?
7 leave a key with the next-door neighbour when you go away?

Now put your ideas into single sentences, using **in case** and **so that**.

Examples It's a good idea to carry an umbrella in Britain **in case** it rains.

> You should carry an umbrella when you go out in Britain | **so that** you don't get wet. / **in case** you get wet.

14.5 JUST IN CASE   Practice

A: You'd better write my address down.
B: Why?
A: Well, you never know. You might want to write me a letter.
B: Oh, that's all right – | I can remember it. |
| I'll telephone you instead. |
A: Well, I think you should write it down anyway, (just) in case | you forget. |
| you want to write. |

Have more conversations. A advises B to:

1 stop for petrol
2 buy some candles
3 have lunch early
4 take a pullover with him/her
5 take a book with him/her to the doctor's
6 take a spare film on holiday with him/her

14.6 ROAD SIGNS: WARNINGS   Practice

Look at the road signs below. What do they mean?

Work in groups of three. This is a game of noughts and crosses.

Students A and B: Indicate which square you want to fill by giving an appropriate warning.

Example You'd better slow down | – the gates might be closed. |
| in case there's a train coming. |

Student C: Listen to students A and B, and mark the noughts and crosses in the right squares.

14.7 GENERAL ADVICE

Free practice

Walking in the mountains is a riskier business than many people think. Here is a notice from a youth hostel in the Scottish Highlands.

Advice to hill-walkers

If you go hill-walking,
leave yourself plenty of time
carry some food with you
listen to the weather forecast
before you start out
wear suitable clothing and boots
take a map and compass
ideally, go in a group of at least
four - never go alone
tell somebody where you are
going
wear a bright-coloured anorak

Work in groups. Discuss exactly why these precautions are necessary, using the expressions in the box.

you should	might	in case
you ought to	if	otherwise
it's best to	so that	
it's a good idea to		

Choose one of the activities below, and:
1 make your own list of the precautions you should take
2 decide why you should take these precautions

going to live in a tropical country   yachting at sea
driving across the Sahara Desert   skiing

Using the notes that you have made, give general advice to other people in the class about the activity you have discussed.

Writing

Write a paragraph of general advice about *either* the activity you discussed
                                                      or   one of your own hobbies

14.8 VISITING BRITAIN

Listening 🔊

You will hear an interview in which someone gives advice to foreign students who want to come to study in Britain. Listen to the interview and answer the questions.

1 If you go to a British Council office abroad and ask them about courses in Britain, which of the following can you expect them to do?
   a) give you a list of courses and some general advice
   b) give you detailed advice on which course to choose
   c) register you for the course you choose

2 The speaker mentions two things a student can do himself to make sure he goes on a course that suits him. What are they?

3 The speaker mentions three kinds of places that offer courses for foreign students. What are they?

4 a) Why is it a good idea to stay with an English family?
   b) Why should you choose your family carefully?

5 Why is it a good idea to bring:
   a) a raincoat?
   b) one or two pullovers?
   c) travellers' cheques?

6 What is the law in Britain about jobs for overseas students?

Writing

Write a leaflet, 100–150 words long, giving advice to students wanting to study in Britain. Write about:

Choosing a course
– British Council
– writing to schools
– other people

Preparations for coming to Britain
– accommodation
– clothes
– money

Unit 14   Summary of language

In this unit you have learnt how to:
– suggest solutions to particular problems
– advise people to take precautions
– give general advice

KEY POINTS

1 *Basic advice structures*
   You **should** take a holiday.
   You **ought to** phone the police.
   Why don't you have a rest?
   You'd better speak to your father about it.
   If I were you, I'd look for a job.

2 *Reporting advice*
   I **advised** him **to** take a holiday.

   I **suggested that** he | **should** phone
   | **phoned** | the police.

3 *Try + -ing*
   Why don't you try ring**ing** them up?
   Have you tried writ**ing** to them?

4 *Reasons for taking precautions*
   You should wash your hands before eating **because** they **might** have germs on them.
   You should wash your hands before eating **in case** they **have** germs on them.

   You should lock the car **because otherwise** someone **might** steal it.

   You should lock the car | **so that** no-one steals it.
   | **in case** someone steals it.

5 *General advice structures*
   If you go sailing, you **should** always take waterproof clothing.

   And | **it's a good idea to** | check the weather forecast before you set out.
   | **it's best to** |

Activities

ROUND EUROPE

Students A, B, C and D: You've decided to take your family on a three-month tour of Europe. You've got a reasonable amount of money, and you're not sure whether to:

1 go from place to place by plane
2 get a 'Round Europe' train ticket
3 go on a European cruise, calling at the major ports
4 hire a car, and drive round Europe yourself.

You decide to consult an airline, the European Railways Association, a shipping company and a car-hire company, to see what advice they have to give.

Group 1: You are consultants for a European airline.
Group 2: You are consultants for the European Railways Association.
Group 3: You are consultants for a shipping company which specialises in luxury cruises round Europe.
Group 4: You are consultants for a well-known car-hire company.

PROCEDURE

Preparation While the travellers think of the questions they want to ask, each group of consultants discusses:
1 what kinds of things the travellers will want to do on their trip
2 the advantages of their means of transport over the others
3 how to advise them what to do
Consultation In turn, each of the four travellers visits each of the four groups of consultants, asks questions and listens to their advice.
Decision Each of the travellers tells the class how he/she is going to travel, and why.

COMPOSITION

Write 150–200 words about one of the following topics.
1 You have just returned from your three-month trip round Europe, and you had a lovely time. Write a letter to a friend, advising him/her to go on a similar holiday.
2 Write a letter to a relative, asking for a loan, and explaining why you need the money.
3 Write a letter to a friend who you haven't seen for a long time. Tell him/her what you and your family are doing these days, and mention anything interesting that has happened recently.

Unit 15 Origin and duration

15.1 ORIGIN AND DURATION

Presentation

You will hear three short dialogues in which people talk about when they started
doing things and how long they've been doing them.
For each dialogue write down:
a) the question beginning with the words given
b) what the speakers say using the words in brackets

Dialogue 1
Question: How long .... ?

Speaker 1:   .... (last term)

Speaker 2:   .... (two years)

Dialogue 2
Question: When .... ?

Speaker 1:   .... (few weeks)

Speaker 2:   .... (1970)

Dialogue 3
Question: How long .... ?

Speaker 1:   .... (six months)

Speaker 2:   .... (a year)

1 a) How do we use the Present Perfect Continuous with **for** and **since**?
   b) How are **for** and **since** different?

2 a) How do we use the Past Simple with **ago** and **in**?
   b) How are **ago** and **in** different?

3 In dialogue 3, why does the speaker say 'have known', and not 'have been knowing'?

Practice

Answer the questions below, and add a sentence using either **for/since** or **ago/in**.

1 Do you play cards? play tennis? play ....?
2 Can you swim? ride a bicycle? ....?
3 Do you know your next-door neighbour? your local butcher? ....?

15.2 ASKING QUESTIONS Practice

Example: *Somebody tells you he's a member of the Labour Party.*

– Really? How long have you been a member?

– Oh yes? | When / How long ago | did you join?

Ask similar questions about the following, using (a) **How long . . .?** (b) **When/How long ago . . .?**

Somebody tells you that:

1 he drives
2 he's got a dog
3 he has piano lessons
4 his parents are divorced
5 there's a telegram for you from Paris

6 there's a new play on at the local theatre
7 he's out of work at the moment
8 his daughter lives in Berlin
9 the children are in bed

15.3 POINTS AND PERIODS Practice

Examples: *I know your sister. (September)*

A: How long have you known her?
B: I've known her since September.
C: (to A) When did he meet her?
A: He met her in September.

I play bridge. (five years)

A: How long have you been playing bridge?
B: I've been playing for five years.
C: (to A) When did he start playing bridge?
A: He started playing five years ago.

Work in threes. Have similar conversations, based on the remarks below. Use the points or periods of time given.

1 I'm engaged now, you know.   (July)
2 I'm writing a novel.   (a few weeks)
3 I go to evening classes.   (three months)
4 I've got a movie camera.   (Christmas)
5 I'm a graduate now.   (a fortnight)
6 My leg's hurting.   (8 o'clock this morning)
7 I know that joke already.   (years and years)

15.4 'SINCE' WITH CLAUSES   Presentation and practice

A: I see you're driving a Volvo these days.
B: Yes, I've been driving a Volvo (**ever**) **since** I crashed my old Rover.
C: Yes, I've had a Volvo (**ever**) **since** I was promoted.
D: Yes, I've been driving a Volvo (**ever**) **since** I gave the Aston Martin to my daughter.

Work in groups. Give as many explanations as you can of why you're:

1 drinking a lot
2 using a walking stick
3 riding a bicycle
4 learning the guitar
5 living with your mother
6 reading *The Times*
7 carrying a gun

15.5 TALKING ABOUT YOURSELVES   Free practice

Work in groups. Find out from the others how long they have been doing and when they started doing things. Talk about:

where they live   interests
friends   work and routine

15.6 THE LAST TIME   Presentation

'... Of course, you can live very cheaply if you know what you're doing. For example, if you go round to someone's house at about 7 o'clock, they'll always invite you to stay for a meal. I haven't bought any food for over a week now. And then there's transport. It's ages since I paid a taxi fare. Why bother, when there are people with cars who can give you a lift? I used to buy my own cigarettes, too – but then I realised that people always offer them around when they have one themselves. I think I last bought a packet of cigarettes, ooh, about two years ago. And I haven't been to a launderette since last September, either ... It's just a matter of taking what's offered to you – and it doesn't do anybody any harm really, does it? ... Oh, by the way, I couldn't just use your phone for a moment, could I? ...'

In the passage there are four sentences which show when the speaker last did things. Write them below.

1 ....

....

2 ....

....

3 ....

....

4 ....

....

Say each of them in *two* other ways.

When did you last oversleep?
How long is it since you last overslept?

I last overslept about three weeks ago.
It's six months since I last overslept.

I haven't overslept | for ages.
| since March.

Work in groups. Ask each other about the following, as in the example.

going swimming	crying
visiting your aunt	losing your temper
having a temperature	going abroad
going out to dinner	going to a wedding
cleaning your windows	playing cowboys and indians

15.8 LAZY DAYS Reading

Unexpected guests are good for you. The phone
rings, the friends you haven't seen for ages are
arriving in a few hours, and you realise with
horror that you haven't changed the sheets in the
5 spare bedroom for months, that all those dirty
dishes have been in the sink since the weekend,
and that you've been wearing the same socks for
three days.
  I wouldn't call myself a particularly lazy
10 person. I work fairly hard, I keep the flat
reasonably clean, and I feel that, when I settle
down for an evening in front of the TV, on the
whole I deserve to put my feet up. And yet there
are so many things that I don't seem to find the
15 energy to do.
  Take, for example, culture. When I came to
live in London five years ago, I was thrilled. 'This
is it,' I said to myself. 'I'm a bus ride away from
the West End theatres. I've got museums and art
20 galleries on my doorstep, and there are a good
300 films to choose from. And all those
exhibitions, concerts. . . .' For the first few
months, I went. I cleaned myself up, wandered
around exhibitions, queued for first nights and
25 enjoyed myself immensely. But somehow all
that's changed. I don't think I've been inside a
theatre since someone gave me tickets for my
birthday six months ago; and the last time I went
to the cinema was to get out of the rain while I
30 was waiting for a bus. I haven't even been to see
The Mousetrap, but that's been running for more
than 30 years, so it can wait a bit longer.
  It's the same with fashion. When I walk along

the street these days, surrounded by people with
extraordinary haircuts and strangely shaped   35
trousers, I feel like a clock that stopped several
hours ago. I've been wearing the same type of
flared jeans since the sixties, although they're
getting more and more difficult to find in the
shops nowadays. And my hair has been covering 40
my ears ever since I left school and was free to
grow it to the then fashionable length. Those
were the days when I used to know the Top Ten
by heart, and rush out to get the latest singles
before anyone else. Those same (now rather   45
scratchy) records are still there on my shelf, with
only a few more recent additions – it's so long
since I last bought a record that I don't even
know what one costs any more. It isn't that I
don't like the current clothes and music: it's just 50
that keeping up with them is too much like hard
work. So whenever I begin to feel uncomfortably
old-fashioned, I just remind myself that even a

stopped clock is right twice a day: the sixties will be back some time.

When those friends rang unexpectedly the other day, I was doing one of those personality quizzes in a fashionable magazine (not mine – someone had left it in my flat). It was called 'How lazy are you?' and it had questions like:

How long ago did you last write to keep in touch with an old friend?   (a) less than a week ago? (b) less than a month ago? (c) more than six months ago? (d) more than a year ago?   and How long have you had your newest pair of shoes?   (a) a month or less? (b) six months or less? (c) more than six months? (d) more than two years?

Luckily, I was too busy to finish it.

1 According to the writer, how are unexpected guests 'good for you'? (line 1)

2 In general, in what ways is the writer:
   a) lazy?
   b) not lazy?

3 Write T(true) or F(false) by each of the following statements.
   a) The writer lives next door to a museum and an art gallery.
   b) He hasn't been to the theatre for six months.
   c) He's got hair over his ears.
   d) Flared jeans were fashionable in the sixties.
   e) He hasn't bought any records since the sixties.
   f) He doesn't like the current clothes and music.

4 Explain the meaning of the following.
   a) thrilled (line 17)
   b) first nights (line 24)
   c) *The Mousetrap* (line 31)
   d) by heart (line 44)
   e) scratchy (line 46)
   f) keep in touch with (line 61)

5 For what reasons did the writer last go to:
   a) the theatre?
   b) the cinema?
   In what way are these two reasons similar?

6 a) Why does the writer 'feel like a clock that stopped several hours ago'? (line 36)
   b) Explain 'even a stopped clock is right twice a day: the sixties will be back some time'. (line 53)

7 a) Why didn't the writer finish the personality quiz?
   b) Why does he say 'luckily'? (line 69)

8 Do you think the writer is lazy?

9 Write five questions for a personality quiz called 'How lazy are you?'

15.9 PERSONALITY QUIZ

Free practice

Work in pairs.

Pair A: You are going to find out from pair B how *careful* they are with their possessions. Work out together what questions you will ask them.

Pair B: You are going to find out from pair A how *fashionable* they are. Work out together what questions you will ask them.

Tell the rest of the class what conclusions you came to about the personalities of the other pair, and give some of your reasons.

Writing

Write a paragraph about yourself, showing that you are (or aren't) *either* lazy *or* careful *or* fashionable.

Unit 15   Summary of language

In this unit you have learnt how to:
– talk about the origin of present situations
– talk about the duration of present situations
– say how long it is since things happened

KEY POINTS

1 *'Origin' structures*
   How long ago did you become a teacher?

   I became a teacher │ a long time **ago.**
                      │ **in** 1968.

   When did he start playing the guitar?

   He started playing │ six months **ago.**
                      │ **in** June.

   How long ago did you buy your cooker?

   We bought it │ a year **ago.**
               │ last year.

2 *'Duration' structures*
   How long have you **been** a teacher?

   I've been a teacher │ **for** a long time.
                          │ **since** 1968.

   How long has he **been** play**ing** the guitar?

   He's been playing │ **for** six months.
                     │ **since** June.

   How long have you **had** your cooker?

   We've had it │ **for** a year.
                   │ **since** last year.

3 *'Since' with clauses*
   He started playing the guitar **when** he got one for his birthday.
   He's been playing the guitar (**ever**) **since** he got one for his birthday.

4 *Negative origin and duration*
   When did you **last** have a meal?
   How long is it since you **last** had a meal?

   I **last** had a meal two days **ago.**

   I **haven't** had a meal │ **for** two days.
                           │ **since** Tuesday.
   It's two days **since I last** had a meal.

Unit 16 Location

16.1 IN, ON & AT

Presentation

Look at the five sets of sentences below.
When do we use (a) **in**? (b) **on**? (c) **at**?

IN There are thousands of fish in the lake.
My coat is in the wardrobe.
There aren't enough chairs in the
      dining room.

IN There are two islands in the lake.
There are some cows in that field.
There's a fountain in the square.

AT There are crowds of people at the lake today.
There's a policeman standing at the corner.
You have to get off at the next stop.
There are new traffic lights at the crossroads.

ON There are pleasure steamers on the lake.
The coffeepot is on the table.
There are pictures on the wall.

ON There's a town on the lake.
Canterbury is on the road to Dover.
There are customs posts on the frontier.

Practice

Decide what you might find . . .

1 in/on a river
2 in/on a bottle
3 in/on a bed
4 on/at a door
5 in/on the grass
6 in/at a swimming pool
7 in/at the corner

Now fill the gaps with **in, on** or **at**.

1 Have you got an electric blanket .... your bed? I've only got a hot-water
   bottle .... mine.
2 There's a ticket machine .... the entrance to the car park.
3 Finchley Road tube station is .... the Bakerloo Line.
4 In summer, there are always flies .... the kitchen ceiling.
5 She spent the day sunbathing .... the swimming pool.
6 My favourite pub is .... the river bank.
7 There's a newspaper shop .... my way to the office.
8 Scott found a Norwegian flag .... the South Pole.
9 There is snow .... Kilimanjaro throughout the year.
10 Tickets must be shown .... the barrier.

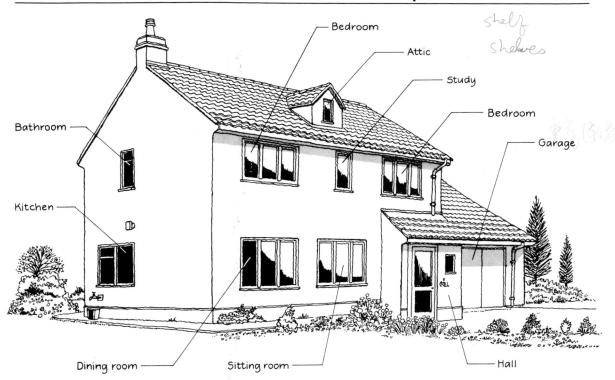

handwritten: shelf / shelves

at the front of	at the side of
at the back of	at the end of
at the top of	at the corner of
at the bottom of	in the middle of

Work in groups. Use the expressions in the box to say where the following are in relation to the house itself.

1 the study   4 the bathroom   7 the chimney
2 the attic   5 the tap   8 the hall
3 the garage   6 the gardens   9 the sitting room

Example The study is **at the front of** the house.

Now talk about them in relation to other parts of the house.
Example The study is **above** the sitting room.
           The study is **between** the two bedrooms.

There's a swimming pool on the roof of the hotel.
The hotel's got a swimming pool on the roof.

There's a fire escape at the side of the hotel.
The hotel's got a fire escape at the side.

There's a flower on the side of the jug.
The jug's got a flower on the side.

There's a crack in the handle of the jug.
The jug's got a crack in the handle.

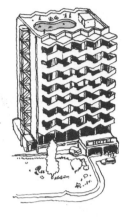

Look at the pictures below. Talk about each one in the same way.

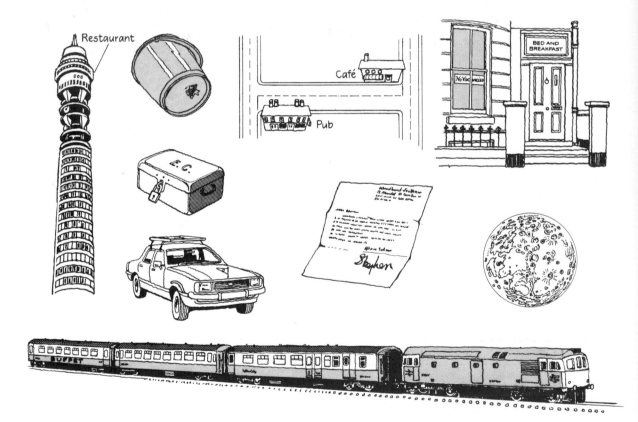

16.4 LOCATION QUIZ   Practice

How many of these questions can you answer?

1 What is special about:
   a) a unicorn?
   b) a centaur?

2 What happens when there is an eclipse of the sun?

3 Describe the flags of:
   a) Japan
   b) America

4 Where would you see the following?

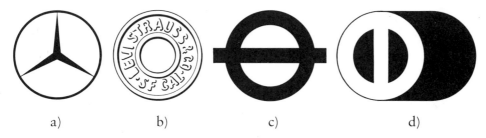

   a)   b)   c)   d)

5 Where would you find:
   a) a stage door?
   b) numberplates?
   c) a filter tip?
   d) a skylight?
   e) a full stop?

6 What is:
   a) a hot dog?
   b) Irish coffee?

7 How do you arrange the 16 men on a chessboard at the beginning of a game of chess?

16.5 DESCRIBING PLACES AND THINGS   Free practice

Work in groups. Describe:

1 the arrangement of rooms and other features in your house or flat
2 an interesting street or park near where you live
3 an interesting ornament or picture that you have at home

16.6 GEOGRAPHICAL LOCATION

Presentation and practice

Look at the maps below, and read the information about Alexandria and Merthyr Tydfil.

Map 1
Alexandria is in North
  Africa.
It's on the southern shore
  of the Mediterranean.
It's on the north coast of
  Egypt.
It's at the mouth of the
  river Nile.
It's northwest of Cairo.

Map 2
Merthyr Tydfil is in South
  Wales.
It's on the southern edge
  of the Brecon Beacons.
It's about 30 miles
  northeast of Swansea,
  on the A465.
It's about 25 miles north
  of Cardiff, on the A470.
It's on the way to Brecon
  from Cardiff.

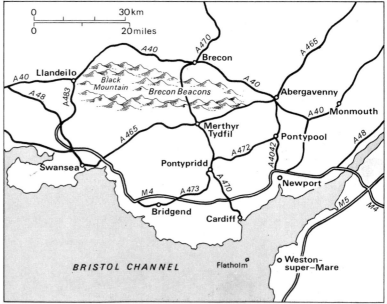

In the same way, describe in as much detail as you can where the following places are:

Map 1

1 Lake Victoria
2 Khartoum
3 Canary Islands
4 Timbuktu
5 Rostov
6 Abadan

Map 2

1 Brecon
2 Bridgend
3 Flatholm
4 Pontypool

Practice

Work in groups. Write down the names of three places whose location you know. Ask the other people in the group to tell you exactly where they are. If they can't tell you, you will have to tell them.

16.7   DESCRIBING COUNTRIES

Free practice

Work in groups. Talk about your own country. Use the checklist below to help you.

Where it is
Which continent is it in?
Which part? Northern, southern, eastern, western?
Is it on a sea or ocean?
Which countries does it border on?

Climate
Where is it hotter? cooler? wetter? drier?

Regions
Where are there mountains? plains? deserts?
Where are there agricultural areas, mining areas, industrial areas, tourist areas?

Features
What important rivers and lakes are there? Where? Other natural features?

Towns
Where is the capital?
Other major towns?

Writing

Write a brief geographical description of your country. Include only important and interesting information.

Listen to the conversation between Susan and Stephen, and answer the questions.

1 What do Susan and Stephen do during the year?

2 How does Susan feel about Stephen's holiday (a) when he first mentions it? (b) at the end?

3 Why isn't Stephen going to Austria or Switzerland?

4 On the map, mark:
a) Aviemore
b) the ski slopes
c) the whisky distilleries

5 How many days will Stephen actually be in Aviemore?

6 What problems might there be with the weather?

7 What will Stephen do if he can't ski?

8 What does he do at the end of the conversation?

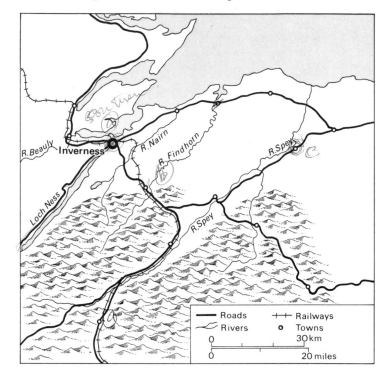

9 Write T(true) or F(false) against these statements:
a) Stephen thinks skiing in Scotland is better than skiing in the Alps.
b) You can't get a suntan at a Scottish skiing resort in winter.
c) Stephen has been planning this trip for a long time. T
d) Stephen has been to Aviemore before.
e) Stephen needn't go to Inverness on his way to Aviemore.
f) Stephen will be staying in a big hotel.

Unit 16 Summary of language

In this unit you have learnt how to:
- say where things and places are
- describe the position of features
- describe countries and regions

KEY POINTS

1 *'In', 'on' and 'at'*
   He was hiding **in** the cupboard.
   I left my car **in** the car park.
   There was a label **on** the bottle.
   The house is **on** the main road.
   He was standing **at** the window.

2 *Phrases indicating precise location*
   My bedroom is **at the back of** the house.
   There's a letter box **at the corner of** our street.
   The freezer is **at the top of** the fridge.
   There was a picture of Elvis Presley **on the cover of** the book.
   Our garden's got trees **at the end**.
   There's a hole **in the knee of** my jeans.

3 *Geographical location*
   Beirut is on the eastern shore of the Mediterranean.
   St Helens is about 12 miles northeast of Liverpool, on the A57.
   New Orleans is on the Gulf of Mexico, at the mouth of the Mississippi.

4 *Vocabulary*
   features of objects
   geographical features

(handwritten notes)
go by the train
5 days returned
get back Friday

Bed & B
Walk in the Loch Ness

Activities

HOLIDAY PICTURES

Work in groups. Bring in *either* a set of postcards from somewhere you've been on holiday *or* some holiday photographs which show some interesting places. Show them to the others in your group, giving them any interesting information about each one. Talk about:

1 where each place is
2 what you did there
3 the tourist attractions and their history
4 the people and what they're doing

Imagine you're on holiday in one of the places you've seen. Write a postcard home.

COMPOSITION

Write 150–200 words on *one* of the following topics.

1 Tell the story of a time when you had a narrow escape.
2 Write a story beginning 'It was 3 o'clock in the morning when the phone woke me up'.
3 Write a story ending 'I never saw her again'.

SITUATIONS

1 During a job interview, the interviewer asks you about your sporting activities. What do you say?
2 A friend's got hiccups. Give her some advice.
3 A friend asks you how long it is since you last had a holiday. What do you say?
4 You're going to the King's Theatre and you've got lost. Ask for directions.
5 A friend invites you to come mountain climbing. Refuse, saying why.
6 While you're in England, someone asks you where you come from. Tell him the name of your town, explaining exactly where it is.
7 Someone's going out with you in a small boat. Advise him to wear a life jacket, explaining why.

Unit 17 Similarities and differences

17.1 DISCOVERING SIMILARITIES Presentation and practice

In the same way, make *two* responses to each of the following remarks:

Work in threes. Use the prompts below to have conversations as in the example.

Example: breakfast A: I had a boiled egg for breakfast.
B: So did I.
C: I had one too.

  1 breakfast
  2 this evening
  3 my dog
  4 Brussels
  5 three times a day
  6 mountain climbing

17.2 SIMILARITIES AND DIFFERENCES   Practice

A: I do a lot of reading.
B: Do you? So do I – I read at least two books a week.
C: Oh, I don't – I never have enough time to read.

Work in groups. Have similar conversations, starting with the remarks below. Each time, add a reason or an explanation, as in the example.

1 I've never eaten caviare.
2 My landlord's very nice.
3 I'd like to see that film again.
4 I didn't sleep very well last night.
5 I'm not very good at skiing.

6 Our neighbours make a lot of noise.
7 I'll have another beer.
8 I prefer driving to being driven.
9 I want to leave here as soon as possible.
10 I love doing exercises in groups.

17.3 THE SAME THING IN A DIFFERENT WAY   Practice

A: I'm so lazy.

B:
| Yes, I'm rather lazy myself.
| Mm, I'm not particularly active myself.
| Well, I don't work very hard myself.

How many replies ending with **myself** can you think of for each of these remarks?

1 I spend all my time at home.
2 God, I feel awful.
3 I usually get up late.
4 I'm a very careless driver.

5 I'm hopeless at English.
6 I walk a lot.
7 I'm always broke.
8 I don't know anything about wine.

17.4 BOTH & NEITHER   Presentation and practice

Work in pairs. Fill in the table below both for yourself and your partner.

Do you: *Yourself* | *Your partner*

1 do a lot of skiing?
2 know how to drive?
3 get up early in the morning?
4 spend a lot of time watching TV?
5 smoke?

Have you ever:

1 been abroad?
2 seen your name in print?
3 been horse riding?
4 been arrested?
5 had a long conversation with an Englishman?

Using the table, tell someone else about yourself and your partner. Tell him/her:
a) what **both** of you do/have done;   b) what **neither** of you does/has done.

Find out what things you **all** do in your class, and what things **none** of you do.
What things do **a few** of you do?   What things do **most** of you do?

17.5   IDENTIFYING FEATURES   Presentation and practice

Work in pairs.

Student A:
Your partner will choose two of the houses below. Try to guess which two he/she has chosen by asking questions like this:

Has **either** of the houses got chimneys?
Does **either** of them have a flat roof?

Student B:
Choose two of the houses below. Your partner will try to guess which two you have chosen. Answer his/her questions like this:

Yes, **one** of them has got chimneys.
Yes, **both** of them have chimneys.
No, **neither** of them has got chimneys.

1

2

3

4

5

6

7

8

9

17.6 TASTES IN COMMON   Free practice

You will hear two women and a man talking about their taste in places for a holiday.
Listen to the tape, and answer the questions.

1 Which of the people have similar tastes in holidays?
2 What kind of places:
   a) does the first woman dislike? Why?
   b) does the man like? Why?
   c) does the second woman like? Why?

Work in groups. Find out:
1 what you have in common with each other
2 who you have most in common with
3 who you have least in common with

Talk about:
taste in places for a holiday
taste in restaurants
taste in clothes
taste in men/women

17.7 CLASSIFYING   Presentation and practice

Which member of this set is the odd man out? Why?
SPIDER   ANT   BUTTERFLY

Spider
Both ants **and** butterflies are insects, **whereas** spiders aren't. Also, **neither** ants **nor** butterflies trap their food, **whereas** spiders do.

Ant
Neither spiders **nor** butterflies live in colonies, **whereas** ants do.

Butterfly
Both ants **and** spiders are carnivorous, **whereas** butterflies aren't.

Look at these other sets. Say why each member can be the odd man out.

1 camera   television set   tape recorder
2 coal   wood   iron
3 Rome   Amsterdam   Venice
4 piano   violin   piano accordion
5 bicycle   train   ship
6 skiing   chess   football
7 coffee   lettuce   tobacco

17.8 SIMILAR BUT DIFFERENT

Free practice

Read this passage about Scotland and Wales, and answer the questions.

Although neither Scotland nor Wales is a truly independent country, both the Scots and the Welsh regard themselves as having a separate nationality and identity, which is certainly not 'English'. Both countries have their own cultural traditions, and also their own language – Welsh in Wales and Gaelic in Scotland. Of the two languages, Welsh is considerably more important: it is spoken by a large number of people and taught in schools all over Wales, whereas Gaelic is spoken by far fewer people, mainly on the West Coast of Scotland.

1 In what ways are Scotland and Wales similar?
2 In what ways are they different?

Work in groups. Choose *either* two areas of your own country
            or   your own country and a neighbouring country

In what ways are they similar?
In what ways are they different?

Writing

Write a paragraph summarising the similarities and differences you have talked about.

Reading

Read this passage, which is from the introduction to an Arabic textbook, and answer the questions.

It is generally thought that Arabic is a single language, spoken, written and understood by people in countries as widely separated as Iraq, Egypt and Morocco, but this is not so. It is only *written* Arabic (that is, the Classical Arabic of the Koran and the Modern Arabic of contemporary literature, journalism and broadcasting), that is more or less common to the whole of the Arab world. The colloquial Arabic which is spoken in the different Arab societies today differs as widely between Arab countries as do Italian, Spanish and Portuguese. In the Arab world, written Arabic acts as a kind of Esperanto, providing a means of communication between educated people of different Arab nationalities. Written Arabic is, paradoxically, spoken too: on the radio and television, in public speeches, as well as between Arabs from different countries. We could call it *pan-Arabic*. It is used in rather the same way as Latin was used by educated people in Europe in the Middle Ages.

Even in English, of course, there are differences of grammar and vocabulary between the written and spoken language, but this difference is far less than that between the artificial pan-Arabic and the living colloquial language of any Arab country. Moreover, both written and spoken English are recognised in English-speaking countries as belonging to one living language, and both are taught in schools. Colloquial Arabic, on the other hand, is not regarded by the people who speak it as 'proper' Arabic. Unlike colloquial English, it is not taught in schools, and it is not written; indeed, there is a strong feeling in Arab societies that it should not be used in a written form.

The educated Egyptian, then, uses pan-Arabic to talk to equally educated Iraqis, Saudis and Moroccans. No reasonable man, however, wishes to talk like a book or a newspaper, and the language that the same educated Egyptian uses with his family and with other Egyptians is quite different. This language is wholly Egyptian, and it is only *spoken*.

(adapted from *Teach Yourself Colloquial Arabic* by T. F. Mitchell, Hodder and Stoughton, 1962)

1 What mistaken view do most people hold about Arabic?

2 The writer mentions *written Arabic*, *Classical Arabic*, *Modern Arabic*, *pan-Arabic*, and *colloquial Arabic*.
   a) Which of these terms mean the same?
   b) What are the differences between them?

3 How is pan-Arabic similar to Esperanto and Latin?

4 What kind of Arabic would an educated Egyptian use for:
   a) making a speech?   c) talking to an Iraqi?
   b) talking to his friends?   d) writing a letter?

5 How are attitudes to colloquial Arabic different from attitudes to colloquial English?

Discussion

1 Why do you think colloquial Arabic is so different from written Arabic?
2 What do you think are (a) the advantages and (b) the disadvantages for Arabs of their language system?
3 In what ways is the Arabic language system similar to/different from the language system in your own country?

Unit 17 Summary of language

In this unit you have learnt how to:
– talk about similarities and differences
– say what you have in common with other people
– say how you are different from other people
– classify things according to similarities and differences

KEY POINTS

1 *Positive and negative 'agreement' structures*
I've got a dog.
I've got one **too**.
So have I.

I enjoyed the film.
I did **too**.
So did I.

I don't like spiders.
I don't like them **either**.
Nor/Neither do I.

I can't sing.
I can't **either**.
Nor/Neither can I.

2 *'Myself'*
I don't like spiders.
No, I'm not very fond of them **myself**.

I enjoyed the film.
Yes, I quite liked it **myself**.

3 *'Both', 'neither', 'either'*
We've **both** been to Canada.
Both of us have been to Canada.

Neither of them knows how to read.
Does **either of** the rooms have a bath?

4 *'Both . . . and . . .' and 'Neither . . . nor . . .'*
Both Iceland **and** Norway are famous for fishing.
Neither tea **nor** coffee is good for you in large quantities.

5 *'Whereas'*
In Mexico they speak Spanish, **whereas** in Brazil they speak Portuguese.

Unit 18 Obligation

18.1 OBLIGATION AND PERMISSION   Presentation

Read the two paragraphs below, and answer the questions.

A
'Your temperature has gone down now, so you needn't stay in bed any longer. You can eat whatever you like, but you mustn't drink any alcohol until you've finished taking the tablets. And you must stay indoors for at least three days. After that you can go out for short walks, but you mustn't do anything too energetic.'

B
'We're allowed to have guests in our rooms, but they have to leave by nine o'clock. And we aren't allowed to have parties – in fact, we can't even have the radio on after seven p.m. At least we don't have to clean our own rooms – there are cleaning ladies who come and do it for us. And we can stay in bed as long as we like, only if we get up after nine o'clock we have to make our own beds.'

Complete these sentences from the two paragraphs:

Obligation
1 A: You .... stay indoors.
   B: We .... make our own beds.
2 A: You .... drink any alcohol.
   B: We .... have parties.

Permission
1 A: You .... eat whatever you like.
   B: We .... have guests in our rooms.
2 A: You .... stay in bed any longer.
   B: We .... clean our own rooms.

Why are the verbs used in the two paragraphs different?

18.2 DOCTOR'S ORDERS   Practice

A is a doctor. B is his patient in hospital. C and D are other patients.

Examples A to B: You | **must** stay in bed. |
                      | **mustn't** get up. |

C to D: Poor B – | he's **got to** stay in bed. |
                 | he's **not allowed to** get up. |

A to B: You | **can** get up now. |
            | **needn't** stay in bed any longer. |

C to D: Lucky B – | he **can** get up now. |
                  | he **doesn't have to** stay in bed any longer. |

Here are some other things the doctor says to B. In groups, talk about them in the same way.

1 You must have an injection every day.
2 You needn't take the tablets any more.
3 You must lie flat on your back.
4 You must drink five litres of water a day.

5 You mustn't talk to anyone.
6 You can go out for short walks.
7 You mustn't smoke.

8 You mustn't move.
9 You mustn't drink.
10 You needn't stay here any more.

18.3 NOTICES   Practice

Look at these notices and explain: a) where you might see them
                                    b) what they mean

Example

> **Final date for applications: 31 December**

This is part of an advertisement for a job. It means:

You have to apply by 31 December.
You can apply any time up to 31 December.
You can't apply after 31 December.

1 **NO PHOTOGRAPHS**

2 Admission: ADULTS 20p, CHILDREN FREE

3   **Barclaycard
Welcome here**

4 **PLEASE ENTER WITHOUT KNOCKING**

5 Not transferable.
Valid on day of issue only.

6 *Evening dress optional*

7 **SILENCE**

8 COME IN AND LOOK AROUND –
NO OBLIGATION TO BUY

9 **EXACT FARE ONLY
NO CHANGE GIVEN**

10 **EMERGENCY EXIT ONLY**

11 Pre-paid envelope
No stamp required

18.4 MAKE & LET

Presentation

Au pair girl: 'The family I'm with is really tyrannical. They make me get up at six in the morning and do all the washing before breakfast. And they don't let me go out in the evening, except on Saturday; and then they make me come home by nine o'clock, which is when they go to bed. At least they don't make me spend all my time with their revolting children – if I haven't got any work to do, they let me sit in my room and read.'

1 What: a) does she have to do?
b) doesn't she have to do?
c) is she allowed to do?
d) isn't she allowed to do?

2 Look back at paragraph B in 18.1, and talk in the same way about the rules of the student hostel, using **make** and **let**.

Practice

Work in groups. Using **make** and **let**, discuss what rules and regulations there are in the following places:
1 an aeroplane
2 the army
3 prison

18.5 PAST OBLIGATIONS   Free practice

Work in groups. Tell each other about your obligations when you were 12 years old.

Say what you: **had to** do
didn't have to do
could and **couldn't** do
were and **weren't allowed to** do

and what your parents **made** and **let** you do.

Talk about:
keeping your room tidy   staying out all night
watching TV   getting up in the morning
washing up   doing your homework
going out in the evening   having boy/girlfriends
earning your own money

18.6 FREEDOM OF CHOICE   Presentation

You will hear a mother talking about the problems she has controlling her children.
Listen to the tape and answer the questions.

1 What two problems do parents have when they make rules?
2 What three things did the speaker's children want to do?
3 What three things can Jack do?
4 What did the speaker decide to do?
5 Why was it successful?

Here are three things that Jack's mother said to Jack. Write *two* other ways of saying each one.
1 You can get up whenever you like.

....

....

2 I don't mind who you play with.

....

....

3 You can drink anything you like.

....

....

Here are three things the speaker said to her children. Write *one* other way of saying each one.
1 You can drink as much wine as you like.

....

2 I don't mind how late you get up.

....

3 You can play with Angela as often as you like.

....

18.7 IT'S UP TO YOU   Practice

Example A: Do I have to sit here?
          B: No, you can sit **wherever you like**.
          C: You can sit **anywhere you like**.
          D: **I don't mind where** you sit.

Work in groups. Answer the questions below in the same way.

Do I have to sit here?   Who shall I bring to the party?
What time should I come?   Shall I bring flowers?
Should I wear a suit/dress?   Do I have to eat fish?
When can I visit you?   When do I have to get up?
How should I dance to this tune?   Should I sleep in this room?
Do I have to drink beer?   Do I have to marry him/her?

Now do these. This time, only give *two* answers.

How late can I stay out?   How much wine can I drink?
How fast can I drive?   How soon can I go home?
How much money can I spend?   How late can I stay in bed?
How often can I come and see you?   How much cheese can I have?

18.8 AWAY FROM HOME

Free practice

getting up   giving parties   using hot water
going to bed   cooking in your room   having the fire on
making noise   using the garden   paying rent
having guests

Pair A: You are renting a room in England, and you want to know exactly what you
         can and can't do, what you have to do and don't have to do. Decide what
         questions you will ask your landlord/landlady, and which things are most
         important for you. Use the list above to help you. Be prepared to argue if
         necessary.
Pair B: You have just let a room to a student, who wants you to tell him or her the
         rules of the house. You are strict about some things, but not about others.
         Decide what your rules are about the items on the list above, and which ones
         you insist on your guests obeying. Be prepared to argue if necessary.

Now form new pairs (one A and one B) and act out the conversation.

Writing

You are the student. Write a letter home describing life in your new accommodation,
based on the conversation you have had.

18.9 COAL MINES

Listening

You will hear someone talking about conditions in coal mines in the early nineteenth century. Listen to the tape and answer the questions.

1 What work did (a) the men (b) the women (c) the children have to do?
  What was particularly unpleasant about each job?
2 a) What did the mine owners make the children do?
  b) What didn't they let them do?
3 The speaker gives two examples of the mine owners' power. What are they?
4 How were the owners able to have such power?
5 Why did people think women shouldn't work in mines?
6 What was the effect of:
  a) the Combination Laws?
  b) miners being allowed to form unions?

Writing

Write a paragraph of 100–150 words, saying what conditions were like in mines at the beginning of the nineteenth century.

Unit 18 Summary of language

In this unit you have learnt how to:
– impose obligation and give permission
– talk about obligation and permission
– talk about rules and regulations
– give complete freedom of choice

KEY POINTS

1 *'Obligation' structures*
   You **must** be home by 9 o'clock.
   You **mustn't** stay out too late.

   We**'ve got to** stay in our seats.
   We **can't/aren't allowed to** walk about.

2 *'Permission' structures*
   You **can** do the washing up later.
   You **needn't/don't need to** do the washing up now.

   We **can** pay by cheque.
   We **don't have to** pay in cash.

3 *'Make' and 'let'*
   At some schools, they **make** you wear a uniform.
   He **doesn't make** his students do enough work.
   They **let** their cat sit on the table.
   Her parents **don't let** her eat sweets.

4 *Habitual obligation and permission in the past*
   They **made** us do the washing-up every morning.
   I **couldn't** have any guests in my room.
   He **didn't have to** get up early on Sundays.
   They **let** us smoke during examinations.

5 *Freedom of choice*
   You can say what**ever you like**.
   You can go **anywhere you like**.
   I don't mind who you invite to dinner.
   You can stay there **as long as you like**.

Activities

THE NEW MOTORWAY

Axeley and Craymouth are important ports. Bridgeport is a picturesque fishing port, which has declined because the estuary has silted up. Dewley is the centre of a mining and industrial area which has declined because of lack of communications. The roads between Axeley, Bridgeport, Craymouth and Dewley are narrow and winding, and cannot take heavy traffic.

You are members of the Regional Council. You are planning to build a motorway from Axeley to Craymouth, to open up the area to industrial and tourist development.

Group A: You are interested in *developing industry* in the region, especially in the area round Dewley.

Group B: You are interested in the *conservation* of the region, especially the National Park, which is an area of outstanding natural beauty.

Group C: You are interested in *developing tourism* in the region, especially around Bridgeport, which could become a centre for skiing in the mountains.

Group D: You are interested in finding the *cheapest route* for the motorway, as the region is short of money.

PROCEDURE

1 In your groups, decide where you think the motorway should be built. Think of arguments to support your point of view.
2 Form new groups (one A, one B, one C and one D). Try to reach agreement about where to build the motorway.

COMPOSITION

Write 150–200 words on one of the following topics.
1 Write a report based on your discussion, saying what you have decided and why.
2 You are a resident in the region. Write a letter to a newspaper, objecting to the decision that has been made.

Unit 19   Prediction

19.1   DEGREES OF PROBABILITY

Presentation

You will hear a conversation between a detective and his chief. Listen to the tape and answer the questions.

1 What has happened? What is happening?
2 Who are: (a) Hammond? (b) Cornfield?
3 The Chief makes a number of predictions about what Hammond will do. Note them down in the correct place in the box below.

He will certainly do this	
He will probably do this	
Perhaps he will do this	*try to get a passport*
He probably won't do this	
He certainly won't do this	*try to leave the country yet*

4 What other prediction expressions does the Chief use, apart from those given in the table?

Practice

Work in pairs. Imagine you are the Detective and his Chief. Using your notes, have conversations as in the example.

Example   Detective: Do you think he'll get in touch with Cornfield?
              Chief: Yes, I expect he'll get in touch with him.

19.2 REASSURING PREDICTIONS   Practice

Don is just going to start doing his national service in the army. He's talking to some friends.

I'm really worried about going into the army.

Don't worry. I expect you'll have a grand time.

Oh, dear. I'm not very fit.

Oh, I doubt if you'll have to go on too many exercises.

I hope they don't make me do anything dangerous.

Well, you never know. You might spend the whole time in an office.

Work in groups. Have similar conversations using the expressions below.

I expect	may	I don't expect
I should think	might	I shouldn't think
	could	I doubt if

You're worried about:

1 an exam you're going to take
2 going on holiday alone
3 having a baby
4 your new job that starts next week
5 going on a blind date

19.3   IF & UNLESS   Practice

Example: Will the price of oil continue to rise?
I'm sure it will go up **if** we carry on using as much oil as we do now.
The price of oil may go down **if** we discover a lot of new oilfields.
Oil prices will certainly continue to rise **unless** we develop solar energy.

Answer these other questions using **if** and **unless**:
1 Will the world's population continue to grow?
2 Will unemployment get worse?
3 Will there be another world war?

Now ask similar questions about things that are in the news.

19.4 WHAT WILL IT BE LIKE?

Free practice

Cordelia is thinking of getting a dog. She wants to know:
1 what she'll have to do
2 what she'll be able to do
3 what she won't be able to do
Tell her what to expect.

Work in pairs. You are thinking of doing one of the things below, and you want to know what it will be like. Decide exactly what you want to know. Then ask your partner.
1 going to live in England
2 going to university
3 taking a holiday job as a waiter/waitress
4 opening a bank account

Writing

Write part of a letter to someone who is thinking of doing one of these things, telling him/her what to expect.

19.5 GOING TO

Presentation

1 a) If I were you, I wouldn't go to England for your summer holiday – it'll probably rain.
 b) Look at those dark clouds – it's probably going to rain.

2 a) You wait and see – she'll leave college, and then she'll get married and have a baby.
 b) She's going to have a baby.

When do we use **going to** in making predictions?

Practice

Look at the remarks below. How does the speaker know what is/isn't going to happen?

1 Something tells me we're going to have sausages for lunch.
2 I don't think we're ever going to get served.
3 Let's get out of here. There's going to be trouble.
4 I think I'm going to be sick.
5 Look out. She's going to faint.

Now look at these pictures. What do you think is going to happen?

19.6 WILL BE DOING & WILL HAVE DONE

Presentation and practice

A scientist working in astrophysics at NASA has just invented a Prediction Machine which can see into the future. This is what the machine tells him about his future.

NOW	1990	2000	2010
Working in astrophysics at NASA	Establishing a colony on Venus	Exploring the galaxy	living in retirement on Titan
↑ invents 'speed of light' spaceship (1988)	↑ marries a Venusian (1995)	↑ Earth explodes (2005)	

In 1989, he **will still be working** at NASA.
By 1989, he **will have invented** a 'speed of light' spaceship.

Now talk about these other dates in the same way:

In 1991 ...   In 1997 ...   In 2001 ...   In 2007 ...   In 2012 ...
By 1991 ...   By 1997 ...   By 2001 ...   By 2007 ...   By 2012 ...

Practice

Work in groups.
1 What do you think you and the others **will be doing** (or **might be doing**):
   a) this time next week?   c) in ten years' time?
   b) next summer?   d) when you're 66?
2 What do you think you and the others **will have done** (or **might have done**):
   a) by this time next week?   c) by the year 2000?
   b) by next summer?   d) by the time you're 66?

19.7 FUTURE DEVELOPMENTS

Free practice

Work in groups. Look at the pictures, which show typical features of present-day life.

To what extent do you think these features will change in the future? For each one say:
1 how things will change
2 why these changes will take place
3 what problems these changes might cause

Writing

Choose one of the topics you have discussed and express your opinion in a paragraph.

Reading

Monsieur Mège-Mourie's invention of margarine was a great advance in technology. After all, it affected one of the most important things in our daily lives – eating. Nevertheless, it has taken
5 margarine more than a century to become a serious rival to butter, and even now it has not won absolute supremacy.

There is no doubt that many similar scientific and technological developments will have taken
10 place by the time the writers of the 2030s sit down to look forward another 50 years to speculate on life in the 2080s. By that time cars may be running on hydrogen taken from the ocean. We may all be living in automatically controlled homes, and
15 carrying portable telephones with us wherever we go. The world's energy crisis may have become history, with the successful application of nuclear fusion. We may be entertained by three-dimensional television, and take two-month
20 holidays. Our education may last until the age of 25, and we may all be living for 120 years. Other, yet unimagined, changes may lie beyond the horizon waiting to take us all by surprise. Whatever form these changes take, the face of life
25 in the future will certainly be significantly different.

Yet, speaking as one who has the advantage of being able to look back more than 50 years, I look forward to the future with confidence, because, in spite of all the changes, I predict that human 30 beings will still be able to exercise choice in deciding how to run their lives.

Looking back 50 years, we can see enormous changes. In the 1930s there were many people in the world who had never seen a car or listened to 35 a radio. A television set was still a technological dream. The moon was untroubled by man and his missiles, and its back was still an unseen mystery. Nuclear reactions existed only in theoretical physics, and to fly the Atlantic from one 40 continent to another was an adventure experienced by few. However, if we were suddenly transported back in time fifty years, I doubt if we would have any great problems settling into the pattern of the everyday life of the 45 1930s.

Similarly, it seems to me that fifty years from now people will choose to keep the principles and values that they have always believed in. New inventions in the future may change the pattern of 50 life, but the human mind that guides it will not alter. Monsieur Mège-Mourie's own nation may be right when they say 'plus ça change, plus c'est la même chose'.*

* 'the more things change, the more they stay the same.'

(from *Our Future* by Magnus Pyke, Hamlyn Paperbacks 1981)

1 What kind of book is *Our Future*?

2 Choose the correct answer. Dr Pyke mentions margarine to make the point that:
   a) technological advances are very important
   b) people are very slow to adapt to new things
   c) artificial things are taking the place of natural things

3 What is Dr Pyke certain about when he talks about the 2030s?

4 In general, what changes does he think we might see by the 2030s in the following fields?
   a) energy   b) work and leisure   c) medicine

5 Imagine you are living in the 1930s and writing a book about the 1980s. Make predictions based on lines 33–42.

6 According to Dr Pyke, in what ways were the 1930s:
   a) very different from the 1980s?
   b) not very different from the 1980s?

7 a) Why does Dr Pyke feel we don't have to worry much about the future?
   b) '*Plus ça change, plus c'est la même chose*' (line 53). How does this apply to the passage? ⟫→

8 Do you think the changes mentioned in lines 12–21 will actually have taken place by the 2030s?

9 Are you as optimistic for the future as Dr Pyke is?

Writing

Summarise the main argument of the passage in about 60 words.
Talk about:
1 the 1930s and the 1980s
2 the 2030s
3 why things won't be so different

Unit 19   *Summary of language*

In this unit you have learnt how to:
– predict future actions and events
– talk about the probability of future events
– talk about particular times in the future

KEY POINTS

1 *Adverbs and modals expressing probability*
   He **will probably/certainly** get in touch with us.
   They **may/might/could** move to a bigger house.
   She **probably/certainly won't** come back before midnight.

2 *Other ways of expressing probability*
   I expect he'll go abroad.
   I shouldn't think she'll be promoted.
   I doubt if he'll get into trouble.

3 *'If' and 'unless' + Present Simple tense*
   The firm may make a profit **if** they attract new customers.
   The firm certainly won't make a profit **unless** they attract new customers.

4 *'Will' and 'going to'*
   Those plants **will** die unless you water them.
   Look at that plant – I think it**'s going to** die.

5 *'Will be doing' and 'will have done'*
   Next summer they**'ll be** living in Berlin.
   By next summer they **will have** moved to Berlin.

Unit 20   Objects

IDENTIFYING TYPES AND FEATURES   **Presentation and practice**

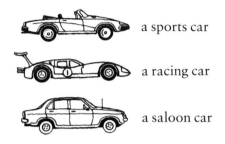

a sports car

a racing car

a saloon car

What types of   (1) clock   (2) boots   (3) fire   (4) knife   (5) bottle   can you see below?

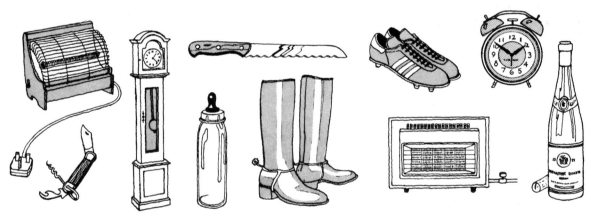

Which of the objects has:

a pendulum   a serrated edge
spurs   a bell
a label   a rubber top
a corkscrew   a pipe
a plug   laces

Work in pairs. Identify each object by talking about something it *has*.

Example   A: Which is the racing car?
            B: It's the one **with** a number on the side.

You will hear a conversation in a lost property office. Write down as much information as you can about the three coats described.

	Type/length	*Colour*	*Other features*
Coat 1			
Coat 2			
Coat 3			

How would you describe the objects below?

Now imagine you are in the lost property office. Have a conversation like the one you heard.

20.3 WHAT DO THEY DO? RELATIVE CLAUSES

Presentation and practice

I went to the Ideal Home Exhibition the other day, looking for a new cooker. I wanted a simple cooker with four rings and an oven, a cooker you light with a match and which then cooks your food. Well, there were lots of cookers that light themselves, and some that turn themselves off when the food's done. I saw cookers you can programme to cook your breakfast while you're still asleep, cookers that turn your chicken for you as it cooks, and even computerised cookers that you can ask for advice. For people in a hurry, there were microwave cookers that will do your dinner in just a few minutes, and for outdoor people, there were some small ones that you can take on picnics and plug into your car battery. I half expected to find a cooker that peels potatoes and cuts them into chips, too. And in all this collection of super-cookers with bells, lights, time-switches and computers, could I find just one that you light with a match?

Not a chance.

'a cooker which cooks your food'
Make a list of the other *relative clauses* that describe *what the cookers do*.
There were cookers ....
....
....
....
....

'a cooker you light with a match'
Make a list of the other *relative clauses* that describe *what you can do with the cookers*.
There were cookers ....
....
....
....

Now talk about some of the other things there were at the Ideal Home Exhibition, using the ideas below.

Example: *Some kettles switch themselves off.*
          There were kettles that switch themselves off.

1 Some coffee percolators keep your coffee hot all day.
2 Some fridges can be fixed on the wall.
3 You can put some glass dishes in a hot oven.
4 Some saucepans stop your milk boiling over.
5 You can defrost some fridges without taking the food out.
6 Some dishwashers can even get the egg off your plates.

Practice

Work in groups. What kinds of things do you think you might find in an Ideal Home Exhibition in five years' time?

Examples: a fridge that can make ice in five minutes
          an electric blanket you can safely leave on all night

A: I've got a watch | with a silver strap.
that tells you the date. |

B: That's nothing. I've got one | that you can wear under water.
with an alarm.
that's got an alarm.
with a gold strap.
that tells you the date and the day. |

Have similar conversations. A has got:
1 a pen that writes in two colours
2 a car with electric windows
3 a chess set that you can put in your pocket
4 a camera with an automatic flash

5 a flat that overlooks the sea
6 a penknife . . .
7 a jacket . . .
8 a dog . . .

20.5 **WEDDING PRESENTS**   Free practice

Work in groups.
Student A: You are going to get married. Three friends want to know what
wedding presents to get you. Tell them exactly what you want.
The others: Each of you is going to buy A a wedding present. Find out exactly what
he/she wants.

Writing

Write a letter to a friend who wants to know what to give you as a wedding present.
Give him/her a choice of three things that you would like.

20.6 OBJECTS WITH A PURPOSE Presentation and practice

A	B	C
sleeping pills	a screwdriver	a message pad
a sewing machine	a dishwasher	paper clips
a riding hat	a fire-extinguisher	photo mounts
a carving knife	a lawn mower	nail varnish
correcting fluid	fly killer	face cream

1 How are the three lists different?
2 Say what each thing is for.

Examples Sleeping pills are pills │ that help you get to sleep.
│ (that) you take when you can't sleep. │

A screwdriver is a tool │ (that) you turn screws with.
│ (that) you use for turning screws. │

Now look at the things below.
What different kinds are there? Which list do they belong to?

brush   paper
opener   basket
glasses   cards

20.7 ASKING FOR THINGS YOU NEED Practice

Look at the remarks below. What is the person asking for in each case?
1 'Have you got a bottle of that white stuff for painting over typing mistakes?'
2 'I need one of those things you use for taking corks out of bottles.'
3 'Do you happen to have one of those gadgets that are used for catching mice?'

You're staying at a friend's house. You find yourself in the following situations,
where you need to ask for something. Ask your friend for them, by explaining what
each thing is for.
1 You've washed your hair and it's still wet.
2 You'd like to clean your shoes.
3 You've bought some lemons and you want to make some lemon juice.
4 Your pencil is blunt.
5 You've spilt some food on your clothes, and there's a greasy stain.
6 You've got some coffee beans and you want to make some coffee.
7 You're setting off on a long overnight drive, and you want to take a hot drink with
   you.

What are the names of the things you have asked for?

20.8 DEFINITIONS QUIZ   Free practice

1 Write down the names of *five* objects you think the other people in your class may not know (e.g. refrigerator, tape recorder, walking stick).

2 Decide how to define these objects.

3 Form groups. Ask questions about your objects, like this:

Q: What do you call a machine that keeps your food cold?
A: A refrigerator.

20.9 A DIFFICULT CHOICE

Listening 🔲

Listen to the passage and answer the questions.

1 a) What relation is the girl to the speaker?
   b) What happened last week?

2 Choose the correct answer. He decided to get her a doll because:
   a) all young girls like dolls
   b) he had known for a long time that she liked dolls
   c) her mother suggested it
   d) the girl asked for it

3 a) What *three* materials were different dolls made of?
   b) Which of them was most common?

4 What two age-groups of dolls were there?

5 What does the speaker say about the dolls' hair?

6 What does he say about their clothes?

7 Write in the missing words:
   And on top of all that, I discovered that there are

   .... and ....

   .... with: .... their eyes when you ....

   ...., dolls hairstyle ...., ... 'mama' (and

   all sorts .... things) when you ...., and dolls

   .... and .... the bed.

8 How long did the speaker stay in the shop?

9 How did he feel during that time? Choose the correct answer.
   a) interested and confused   c) bored and confused
   b) interested and amused   d) bored and amused

Writing

Write a short paragraph describing the doll the speaker bought, in your own words.
Say what it's like, what it has got, what it does, and what you can do with it.

Unit 20   *Summary of language*

In this unit you have learnt how to:
– classify objects into types
– identify and classify objects by their features
– classify objects according to their purpose
– give definitions of objects

KEY POINTS

1 *Compound noun phrases*
   a sports car   a racing car   a lawn mower
   an alarm clock   a sewing machine   a screwdriver
   nail varnish   writing paper   fly killer

2 *Structures for indicating features*

My coat is **the one** | **with** / **that has** | a silk lining.

His skis are **the ones** | **with** / **that have** | silver tips.

He's got a watch **with** a luminous dial.
I've got **one with** a square face.

3 *Subject and object defining relative clauses*
   He's got a gun **that** fires 20 rounds a second.
   I'm looking for a pen **that** will write on glass.

   I want a dish (**that**) you can put in a hot oven.
   A carving knife is a knife (**that**) you carve meat with.

4 *'Use for . . -ing . .'*
   A typewriter is a machine (**you use**) for typing letters.
   What do you call that white stuff (**you use**) **for** washing clothes?
   Glue **is used for** sticking things together.

Activities

CALL MY BLUFF

1 You will hear three definitions of a word that you don't know. Listen to the tape, and vote on which definition you think is the correct one.

2 Work in groups of three. Your teacher will give you a piece of paper with a word on it and the correct definition.

Student A: You will give the true definition of the word. Work out how you will define it.

Students B and C: *Invent* two false meanings of the word, and work out how to define them.

3 When it is your turn, each tell your own definition of the word to the rest of the class. They will vote on which definition is correct.

COMPOSITION

Choose one of the topics below, and write a newspaper article (150–200 words) about it. Write about:
a) its impact on people's lives
b) recent developments
c) possible future developments

1 Electronic games
2 Video machines
3 Nuclear weapons
4 Plastic surgery

SITUATIONS

1 A friend is very worried about an interview tomorrow. Reassure her.
2 You are late for class. Apologise to the teacher and explain why.
3 You are allergic to tobacco smoke. A visitor lights a cigarette in your house. Ask him not to smoke, and explain why.
4 A friend says to you 'You're looking very pleased with yourself'. Tell her why.
5 Your 8-year-old brother asks you 'What's a polaroid camera?' Give him an answer.
6 Someone asks you if you have anything in common with your brother/sister. What do you say?
7 You left your car in a side street, and when you came back you found it wasn't there. Tell the police what happened and what the car looks like.

Unit 21   Degree

21.1   TOO & ENOUGH   Presentation

Letter smuggled out of prison:

> It's dreadful in here. There are six of us in each cell, and no heating at all. You can imagine what it's like at night, with only 2 thin blankets each. "Breakfast" is at 5.30 – watery soup. Then we sit sewing mailbags for 16 hours – without a break, except for half an hour's exercise in the yard. Then more watery soup, and the lights go out at 8.30. Not that it makes any difference – the prison library's only got about 30 books anyway. I don't know if I can

Say what is wrong with conditions in the prison, using **too** and **enough**.

Examples   The cells are **too** crowded.
The cells **aren't** big **enough**.

The prisoners work **too many** hours a day.
They have to do **too much** work.
They **don't** get **enough** free time.

21.2   THE WRONG MAN FOR THE JOB   Practice

Look at the list below of adjectives that describe people. Write in the noun forms.

patient	*patience*
ambitious	
strong	
tactful	
imaginative	
courageous	
intelligent	
dedicated	

Work in threes.
Example   A: I'm going to be a paratrooper.
          B: Nonsense – you aren't courageous enough to be a paratrooper.
          C: And you haven't got enough strength either.

Talk in the same way about these jobs:

1 teacher	4 novelist	7 weightlifter
2 explorer	5 marriage guidance counsellor	8 ....
3 politician	6 spy	

21.3 LINKING SENTENCES   Presentation and practice

Examples: *He can't climb the stairs. He's too weak.*
He's **too** weak **to** climb the stairs.
He **isn't** strong **enough** to climb the stairs.

You couldn't read that book in one evening. It's too long.
That book is **too** long **to** read in one evening.
That book **isn't** short **enough to** read in one evening.

The doorway was too narrow. The piano wouldn't go through.
The doorway was **too** narrow **for** the piano **to** go through.
The doorway **wasn't** wide **enough for** the piano **to** go through.

Work in groups. Make two sentences for each of the following (a) using **too** (b) using
not . . . enough. Use **for** only where it is necessary.

1 We arrived late. We couldn't get any dinner.
2 Don't get married yet. You're too young.
3 You can't drink wine every day. It's expensive.
4 My mother's shopping basket was very heavy. She couldn't carry it.
5 Don't eat that bread. It's stale.
6 We couldn't see through the windows. They were dirty.
7 The stream was too wide. Dad couldn't jump across it.
8 You'd better not sit on the ground. It's damp.
9 You could never wear those trousers in winter. They're too thin.
10 He spoke very fast. I couldn't understand him.

21.4 USELESS POSSESSIONS   Practice

You never throw things away, so your flat is full of things which you have kept, and
you don't know what to do with them. You are talking to a friend.

> You: Oh dear. What shall I do with these gloves?
> Friend: Why don't you wear them for gardening?
> You: Oh, | they're much too good to wear for gardening.
> | they aren't nearly old enough to wear for gardening.

How might you reply to these other suggestions?

Why don't you | give them to your mother?
              | wear them for driving?
              | sell them?
              | wear them in the winter?

Work in groups. Have similar conversations about these other objects:

jeans   photograph   books
coat   clock   sandals
doll

21.5 FAULTS AND REMEDIES

Free practice

You will hear two people talking about education in Britain. Listen to the tape and answer the questions.

1 What does the woman think is wrong with education in Britain?
2 What does the man think is wrong with education in Britain?
3 What does the woman think should be done?

Work in groups. Discuss *one* of the topics below. Say:
a) what you think is wrong
b) what you think | should be / ought to be | done

1 leisure facilities in your area   3 local transport services
2 your school   4 TV programmes

Writing

Write a paragraph expressing your opinion about the topic you discussed.

21.6 SO & SUCH   Presentation

Ali went on a very cheap students' flight to London, but he soon started regretting it:

A He had to wait **so** long at the airport that he felt tired before the journey even started. The flight was **so** bumpy that he felt sick. The plane's engines were **so** noisy that he couldn't hear himself speak. The food was **so** bad that he couldn't eat it.

B He had to wait **such** a long time at the airport that he felt tired before the journey even started. It was **such** a bumpy flight that he felt sick. The plane had **such** noisy engines that he couldn't hear himself speak. They served **such** bad food that he couldn't eat it.

C There were **so** many people on the plane that some of them had to stand. There was **so** little room between the seats that he couldn't stretch his legs.

What kind of words follow **such**, and what kind of words follow **so**?

Add **so** or **such** or **such a** to these words and phrases.

lovely	hard	bad weather	little money
lovely day	hard work	much rain	small amount of money
long time	bad	deep snow	good food
many times	disaster	deep	good meal
pity	disastrous	lot of people	
bad mistake	expensive	many presents	
few people	expensively	expensive presents	

Work in groups of three. You are students A, B and C. Read through your own section only, and then play the game, starting with student A.

Example: He worked very hard for his exams.

      A: He worked so hard for his exams . . .

      B or C: . . . that he almost had a nervous breakdown.

Student A

Change sentences 1–5 into *half-sentences* using **so** or **such**. Students B and C will complete them.

1 He worked very hard for his exams.
2 She looks quite different wearing a wig.
3 He treated his wife badly.
4 It was a very boring film.
5 I've got very few possessions.

Choose one of these sentences to complete what other people in your group read out. Begin with **that**.

. . . I'm not going to eat there again.
. . . taxi drivers refuse to take you there.
. . . we didn't go bathing once.
. . . I have to have my shoes made specially.
. . . even a child could have solved it.
. . . nobody understood him.
. . . my hands were shaking.
. . . he collapsed on the floor.
. . . they appointed a new transport manager.
. . . I decided to walk instead.

Student C

Change sentences 1–5 into *half-sentences* using **so** and **such**. Students A and B will complete them.

1 There was a very long queue at the bus stop.
2 I'd drunk a lot of coffee.
3 The problem was very simple.
4 I have enormous feet.
5 He drank a lot of whisky.

Choose one of these sentences to complete what other people in your group read out. Begin with **that**.

. . . we left half way through.
. . . nobody understood him.
. . . I'm not going to eat there again.
. . . in the end she poisoned him.
. . . they appointed a new transport manager.
. . . I didn't recognise her at first.
. . . he almost had a nervous breakdown.
. . . we didn't go bathing once.
. . . taxi drivers refuse to take you there.
. . . I only need one suitcase when I move.

Student B

Change sentences 1–5 into *half-sentences* using **so** or **such**. Students A and C will complete them.

1 The sea was very cold while we were there.
2 I've heard terrible stories about that restaurant.
3 A lot of people complained about the city bus services.
4 Some parts of New York are quite dangerous.
5 He spoke very fast.

Choose one of these sentences to complete what other people in your group read out. Begin with **that**.

. . . I didn't recognise her at first.
. . . even a child could have solved it.
. . . we left half way through.
. . . my hands were shaking.
. . . I only need one suitcase when I move.
. . . I decided to walk instead.
. . . he collapsed on the floor.
. . . I have to have my shoes made specially.
. . . he almost had a nervous breakdown.
. . . in the end she poisoned him.

21.8 HOLIDAYS

Practice

B has just been to London. A is asking him about it.

Example A: Did it rain very much while you were there?
　　　　　B: Yes, it did. In fact, it rained so much that I had to stay indoors all the
　　　　　　 time.
　　　　　　 or
　　　　　　 No, it didn't. In fact it was such nice weather that I got quite brown.

Have similar conversations, using these ideas:

food good?	hotel clean?	meet people?
many foreigners?	clothes cheap?	speak English?
go out a lot?	travel much?	buy books?

Free practice

Work in groups. Talk about a real holiday you had recently. Use any of the language
you have learnt in this unit where you think it is appropriate.

21.9 THE UGLY NATURE OF EARTH'S TWIN SISTER

Reading

Read the newspaper article below and answer the questions.

Venus wouldn't be a comfortable planet to live on: it's hot enough to melt lead, the air is thick enough to swim in, and there are never-ending electrical storms. V. Axel Firsoff lifts a corner of the veil which covers Earth's neighbour.

5

Venus is closer to the Sun than the Earth is, and the sunlight reaching Venus is twice as powerful as that reaching the Earth. However, it has also been found that Venus,
10 which is covered in thick cloud, reflects twice as much sunlight as the Earth does. So it is quite possible to imagine that Venus might not be too hot to support life, and even to picture it as the home of fair-haired
15 Venusians chasing across the planet in flying saucers.

Unfortunately, this attractive idea does not stand up to close examination. Instead of spinning anti-clockwise like most other
20 planets, Venus revolves clockwise, and it turns so slowly that the sun rises in the west and sets in the east 59 days later. This means that during the immensely long Venusian 'day', the temperature has time to
25 reach 450 degrees Centigrade, easily hot enough to melt tin or lead. Moreover, the polar axis is almost vertical, so there are no seasons.

30 But the real shock comes when we consider the atmosphere. Normally you expect that the closer a planet is to the Sun, the less atmosphere it will be able to retain. Venus, however, has an atmosphere about
35 100 times as dense as ours. The air is much too thick to run in, and a swimming stroke would help you walk in it. On the other hand, the atmosphere is so thick that you could fly through it without any problem.
40 The winds are very slow—the Russian spacecraft Venera 10 measured on landing a maximum air flow of seven miles per hour—yet the atmosphere is so dense that a seven mile per hour wind would be strong enough
45 to knock down a tall building.

Most of Venus is permanently covered in clouds of sulphur and sulphuric acid, and these clouds absorb so much of the Sun's light that on the surface of the planet there is no more than a dark reddish gloom. The
50 Russian spacecraft Venera 9 and 10 found that there was enough light to take TV pictures—this light, however, came not from

⟫⟫→

the Sun but from flashes of lightning given off by continual electrical storms.

All in all, then, Venus turns out to be a dramatic though extremely inhospitable place, and, along with Mars, Jupiter and Saturn, has to be added to the list of planets that are quite incapable of supporting human life.

(adapted from an article by V. Axel Firsoff in *The Guardian*)

1 a) Why might you expect the surface of Venus to be fairly cool?
  b) Why in fact is the surface of Venus hot?

2 If you tried to walk on Venus, what problems would you have?

3 a) Why might you expect the surface of Venus to be bright?
  b) Why in fact is there very little sunlight on the surface?
  c) How did the Russians manage to take TV pictures?

4 What is the most unusual thing about Venus compared with other planets?

5 Explain the meaning of the following:
  a) retain (line 32)   d) absorb (line 47)
  b) dense (lines 34 and 42)   e) gloom (line 49)
  c) swimming stroke (line 35)   f) inhospitable (line 56)

6 'V. Axel Firsoff lifts a corner of the veil which covers Earth's neighbour.' What different things does this sentence suggest about Venus?

7 If Venusians existed, what would you imagine them to be like?

Writing

In a paragraph (about 100 words), compare conditions on Venus with those on Earth, and explain why they are different.

Talk about:
light
heat
atmosphere

Unit 21   Summary of language

In this unit you have learnt how to:
– talk about excess and inadequacy
– say what is wrong with things
– express degree by talking about results

KEY POINTS

1 *'Too' and 'enough'*
   The classrooms are **too** cold in winter.
   The classrooms are**n't** warm **enough** in winter.

   There are **too many** American films on TV.
   There are**n't enough** educational programmes on TV.

2 *'Too' and 'enough' + infinitive*
   I feel **too** tired **to** go out this evening.
   The water was much **too** dirty **to** swim in.
   The office is **too** busy **for** me **to** take any time off.

   He's **not** nearly old **enough to** get married.
   The ice is**n't** thick **enough to** walk on.
   There is**n't enough** food **for** everyone **to** eat.

3 *'So' and 'such'*
   The hotel was **so** comfortable **that** we stayed another week.
   It was **such a** bad film **that** we left half way through.
   He has **so many** children **that** he can't remember all their names.

Unit 22 Setting a scene

22.1 SETTING A SCENE Presentation 🔲

You will hear two extracts from a novel in which the writer sets a scene.

EXTRACT 1

1 What were the following doing?
   a) the tourists
   b) the Englishmen
   c) the children
   d) the girl
2 What was there in the bay? What was it doing?
3 a) What did Jason do?
   b) What do you think he did next?

EXTRACT 2

1 What were the following doing?
   a) the paint
   b) the children
   c) the donkey
2 Who was there outside a café? What were they doing?
3 Exactly what is said about
   a) the houses?
   b) the dusty road?
   c) the statue?
4 a) What did Jacqueline do?
   b) What do you think she did next?

22.2 TEMPORARY ACTIVITIES AND PERMANENT FEATURES Practice

Notice the different forms of the verb *run* in these sentences:

It was a lovely place: a small stream **ran** past the end of the back garden.
She looked out of the window – a small boy **was running** towards the house.

Fill the gaps in the sentences below with the correct form of one of the verbs given.
Use each verb twice.

cross   lie   stand   face   flow

1 An elderly woman who .... the road was knocked down by a motorcyclist.
2 The village .... at the foot of the mountain.
3 The river which .... through the town was polluted.
4 We stopped to ask a policeman who .... on the corner.
5 We stopped to admire the view from the bridge which .... the river.
6 A large oak tree .... in the garden, casting its shade over the house.
7 Although it was rather cold, a few people .... on the beach, sunbathing.
8 The hotel could only offer me a small dark room that .... north.
9 Because of the heavy rain, the river .... much faster than normal.
10 He couldn't see me because he .... the other way.

Imagine that you saw these scenes recently, and that you're telling a friend what you saw.

What could you say about the position of each of the people?
Example The old woman was standing by a fire.

Now describe each scene more fully, as in the examples.

Examples There was an old woman, dressed in a traditional long skirt and a woollen shawl, standing by a fire.
There was a man leaning on a stick, watching the traffic go by.
The sun was going down behind the hills.

Work in groups. Now imagine you saw one of the scenes below while you were on holiday recently. Tell the others what you saw.

22.4 STRIKING SCENES   Free practice

Work in groups. Think of a scene you saw recently that struck you as
    either very beautiful
    or very unusual.
Describe the scene to the others in as much detail as you can.

22.5 THE PAST PERFECT TENSE

Presentation

Read the description below, and answer the questions.

Everything was ready for the party. The room was spotlessly clean, the furniture had
been moved to one side, and the floor at one end of the room was bare, ready for
dancing. There were some open bottles of wine and some food on the table, and
plates and cutlery were laid out neatly on the white tablecloth.

  The host had put on his new white suit. He looked around him with satisfaction.
The atmosphere was just right – he had turned the main lights off and had lit candles
round the sides of the room. A jazz record was playing, and a fire was burning
brightly in the grate . . .

1 In the passage, what is the Past Perfect
 tense used for?

2 Use the Past Perfect to talk about:
 a) the room
 b) the carpet
 c) the bottles of wine
 d) the food
 e) the plates and cutlery
 f) the record
 g) the fire

3 Use the Past (Simple or Continuous) to
 talk about:
 a) the furniture
 b) the lights
 c) the suit
 d) the candles

Practice

Later that evening, the party
got completely out of hand,
and a neighbour called the
police.

By the time they got there . . .

A
. . . everyone in the street was awake.
. . . there was no glass in the windows.
. . . the host was lying unconscious in the hall.
. . . the building was on fire.
. . . the fire brigade was already there.
. . . only a few guests were still there.
. . . the stereo equipment was missing.
. . . the lift wasn't working.
. . . there was a man on the roof.

B
. . . everyone in the street **had woken up.**

The sentences in Column A tell you *how things were*. Complete Column B with
alternative sentences which say *what had happened*.

22.6 PREVIOUS EVENTS

Practice

Work in groups. Look at the sentences below. What things do you think *had
happened* previously?

1 When I returned home for the holidays I found that my parents had made all sorts
   of changes to the house . . .
2 At nine o'clock that morning we were almost ready to set off for our day in the
   country . . .
3 The summer season was over by the time they reached the island . . .
4 The play was about to begin . . .
5 I was in a panic. My guests were due to arrive in two hours, and nothing was ready . . .

Writing

Choose two of the sentences and develop them into paragraphs.

22.7 MEMORIES   Free practice 🔲

You will hear someone describing how he first met his wife.
Listen to the tape and answer the questions.
1 Why was the speaker at the party?
2 How was he feeling? Why?
3 What was the girl doing?
4 How exactly did they meet?

Work in groups.
Tell the others *either* how you first met someone you know very well
           or your earliest childhood memory
           or a dream you remember

22.8 MORNING CALL

Reading

Read the passage below and answer the questions.

I was walking along the deserted main street of a small seaside town in the north of England looking for somewhere to make a phone call. My car had broken down outside the town and I
5 wanted to contact the AA. The street ran parallel to the sea and was joined to it by a number of narrow side streets. Low grey clouds were drifting across the sky and there was a cold damp wind blowing off the sea which nearly threw me off my
10 feet every time I crossed one of the side streets. It had rained in the night and water was dripping from the bare trees that lined the street. I was glad that I was wearing a thick coat.

There was no sign of a call box, nor was there
15 anyone at that early hour whom I could ask. I had thought I might find a shop open selling the Sunday papers or a milkman doing his rounds, but the town was completely dead. The only living creature I saw was a thin frightened cat
20 which was hopelessly sniffing at some empty paper bags that had been dropped outside the fish-and-chip shop the night before.

Then suddenly I found what I was looking for. There was a small post office, and almost hidden from sight in a dark alley next to it was the 25 town's only public call box, which badly needed a coat of paint. I hurried forward, but stopped in astonishment when I saw through the dirty glass that it was already occupied. There was a man inside. He was very fat, and was wearing a cheap 30 blue plastic raincoat and rubber boots. I could not see his face – he was bending forward over the phone with his enormous back pressed against the glass and did not even raise his head at the sound of my approaching footsteps. 35 Discreetly, I remained standing a few feet away and lit a cigarette to wait my turn. It was when I threw the dead match on the ground that I noticed something bright red trickling from under the call box door. 40

1 Find expressions in the passage (as many as you can) which tell you:
   a) that it was early morning
   b) that the weather was dull and very windy
   c) that it was winter
   d) that the town was neglected

2 What is the AA (line 5), and what would they do if the writer phoned them?

3 The writer mentions *three* permanent features of the street she was walking down. What were they?

4 a) Why was the cat sniffing at the paper bags? (line 20)
   b) Why was it sniffing 'hopelessly'?
   c) Why did the writer 'stop in astonishment'? (line 27)
   d) Why did she wait 'discreetly'? (line 36)
   e) What is the difference between 'drip' (line 11) and 'trickle' (line 39)?

5 a) Why didn't the man raise his head when the writer approached?
   b) Why didn't the writer realise immediately that something was wrong?

Free practice

The writer is being questioned by the police, who want to know:
1 why she was in the town
2 what she was doing

3 how she discovered the man
4 exactly what she saw

Student A: You are the policeman. Question the writer in as much detail as you can. Make sure she can prove she is innocent.

Student B: You are the writer. Give an account of your actions, without looking at the text.

Unit 22 Summary of language

In this unit you have learnt how to:
– describe scenes you saw in the past
– talk about previous events
– set the scene for a story

KEY POINTS

1 *Past Continuous structures*
Some children **were** play**ing** in the street.
There were a few people danc**ing**.
There was a man sitt**ing** in the corner, read**ing** a book.

2 *Participle structures*
They were sitting talk**ing** to each other.
He was lying stretch**ed** out in the sun.
An old woman dress**ed** in black was walking down the road.

3 *Past Simple tense for permanent features*
The trees **stood** in a long line beside the road.
The road **crossed** a stream and then **ran** through a forest.

4 *Past states resulting from previous events*
When I got back, I found that everything **was** different.
When I got back, I found that everything **had** chang**ed**.

There **was** some milk in the fridge.
She **had left** some milk in the fridge.

Activities

ESKIMOS

An Eskimo who has never been near a city or a road in his life visits a big city. He sees lots of things he has never seen before. When he gets back home, he describes some of these unfamiliar things to his friends . . .

1 You will hear the Eskimo describe one of the things he has seen in the city. Listen to the tape, and then try to guess what he has described.
2 Work in groups. Think of another familiar thing that the Eskimo saw in the city. Imagine you are the Eskimo, and work out how to describe it to your friends.
3 Describe your object to the rest of the class. They will try to guess what you have described.

COMPOSITION

Below are the first and last sentences of some paragraphs that set a scene for a story. Choose one of the scenes and write:
a) a paragraph describing the scene
b) a second paragraph continuing the story.
Write 150–200 words.

1 When Jane got to the airport building, she found that it was swarming with people . . .
   . . . Jane pushed her way through the crowd towards the information desk.

2 Brian unpacked his suitcase, and looked down from the hotel window to the square below; it was the busiest time of the day . . .
   . . . 'What a nice change from London,' he thought to himself.

3 On board the liner, there was no reason to believe that anything was wrong at all . . .
   . . . In fact, for everyone on board it seemed to be just a normal, calm, sunny day.

Unit 23 Criticising

23.1 WHAT'S WRONG? Presentation and practice

Look at the pictures. What can you find to criticise about the things and people in the pictures? Talk about them using **should**.

Examples The children **shouldn't be skipping** near the clothes line.
There should be a clear notice saying 'Danger' near the lake.
The children **should be playing** football in a park, not in the road.

23.2 SHOULD & IF

Presentation and practice

Colin has a café.

The windows are filthy.
He overcooks everything.
The paint's peeling off.
He doesn't advertise.
He overcharges.
He closes at lunchtime.
He keeps three cats in the café.
He often loses his temper.

He doesn't do very good business.

What **should** (or **shouldn't**) he do? What particular things **would** (or **wouldn't**) happen as a result?

Practice

Work in groups.

A: I don't seem to be able to make any friends.

B: It's your own fault. You | **should** go out more.
| **shouldn't** stay indoors all day.

C: Yes, **if** you went out more, you'd meet a few people.

Have similar conversations, using the situations below.

A always fails his/her exams A gets enormous electricity bills
A feels completely exhausted A never has enough money
A can't sleep A keeps losing things
A can't get a job A never gets invited out

23.3 IRRITATING BEHAVIOUR

Presentation and practice

How would you describe a person who is:

vain absent-minded a gossip
jealous inquisitive a bore
clumsy aggressive a pessimist

Example A vain person is a person who | **is always** | **admiring** himself.
| **keeps**

Writing

George is incredibly vain. He keeps buying new clothes, he's always combing his hair, and he's continually flicking specks of dust off his jacket. And he's constantly looking at himself in shop windows.

Choose three of the characteristics in the list, and write similar paragraphs.

23.4 RECRIMINATIONS   Free practice

Pair A: You are getting fed up with your roommate, because you think he/she:
    is too untidy   doesn't do enough housework
    is very unsociable   doesn't go out enough

You've decided to have a serious talk with him/her. Decide what particular things he/she keeps doing that annoy you, and prepare what you will say to him/her.

Pair B: You are getting fed up with your roommate, because you think he/she:
    has too many friends to stay   is too noisy
    is too fussy about the flat   does too much cooking

You've decided to have a serious talk with him/her. Decide what particular things he/she keeps doing that annoy you, and prepare what you will say to him/her.

Now form new pairs (one A and one B) and act out the conversation.

23.5 PAST MISTAKES   Presentation and practice

You will hear a conversation between a burglar and a detective. Listen to the tape, and answer the questions.

1 Why is the burglar being arrested?

2 What *five* mistakes did he make? What happened as a result of each one?

Mistake	*Result*

⋙→

3 Talk about each of the mistakes using **should** or **shouldn't**.

4 What **would** (or **wouldn't**) **have happened** if he hadn't made each mistake?

5 What does he think the detective
   a) shouldn't have done?
   b) should have done?

6 Here are some other mistakes that the burglar made. Criticise him for each, and explain your criticism using 'If . . .'

He boasted about the robbery in a pub.
He went straight home after the robbery.
He didn't wait until dark.
He didn't sell the jewels.
He became a burglar.

23.6 EVENTS AND CIRCUMSTANCES

Presentation and practice

Example: The boat overturned. Colin wasn't wearing a life jacket.

He drowned.
He should have been wearing a life jacket.
If **he'd been wearing** a life jacket, **he wouldn't have drowned.**

Look at the situations below. For each one:
a) say what you think happened as a result
b) say what the person should(n't) have been doing
c) explain your criticism using 'If . . .'

1 A man stepped out in front of Basil's car. Basil wasn't concentrating on his driving.
2 Linda's fiancé walked in. Linda was kissing the electrician.
3 Dick was smoking in bed. He fell asleep.
4 The baby picked up a worm. Agnes wasn't watching the baby.
5 The fire alarm went off. Phil was wearing his headphones.

Practice

Example: Fred has an awful cold.

A: Poor old Fred. He's got an awful cold.
B: It's his own fault: he shouldn't have gone for that long walk in the rain.
C: And he should have been wearing a raincoat.
D: He should have changed his clothes when he got home, too.
E: And he . . .

What other criticisms could you make about Fred?

Work in groups. Have similar conversations about the following people. Think of as many criticisms as you can.

1 Ann was nearly run over on a country lane last night.
2 Jack was arrested yesterday.
3 George has been shot in the leg.
4 Clare failed her interview.
5 Keith was bitten by a dog last week.

Reading

Carnival violence—what went wrong?

The violence at last weekend's Caribbean Carnival has raised a storm of controversy throughout the country, and has led to strong criticism of the different groups involved.

Although the Carnival has been free of violence in recent years, this year the police had expected some trouble, and were present in large numbers. The extreme right-wing National Front had threatened to stage a demonstration if the Carnival went ahead, and some white residents had demanded that the Carnival should be banned.

The fighting apparently started in a café, when a West Indian threatened two National Front members, who, he claimed later, had insulted him. Police moved in, and minutes later the street was a raging battleground, as mainly black youths threw bottles, and broke shop windows.

The National Front staged a noisy demonstration nearby, but police managed to keep the two groups separate. However, it was after midnight before the situation was brought under control, and by then at least 50 arrests had been made, and several people, including police, had been taken to hospital.

So who was to blame? Could the violence have been avoided? We have been asking some of those involved for their views.

Police Spokesman: We tried to stay in the background by keeping to the side streets, but there's a lot of tension in the area, and we had a duty to have enough men there to deal with any trouble that might occur. What happened on Sunday has shown that this was absolutely the right decision. If we hadn't been there, the violence would have been much worse than it was.

Carnival Organiser: Everyone was enjoying themselves until the police moved in. The incident in the café wasn't very serious, and I think the police sparked off the violence by over-reacting. They should have just stayed where they were. If they'd kept out, things would've quietened down. You just don't need 800 policemen to control a carnival—having police vans round every corner just made everyone feel there was a lot of tension about.

National Front Spokesman: This is a free country and we can express our views wherever we like. We don't like blacks living in this area, and we don't like them holding their foreign carnival in our streets. We demonstrated peacefully—it was the blacks that started the violence, not us. We said long ago that the Carnival should be banned—if our advice had been taken, none of this would have happened.

Local resident: The National Front should never have been allowed to go near the Carnival. Blacks and whites live together here quite happily and we enjoy our Carnival. The National Front shouldn't be allowed to come here and upset everyone. Most of the kids who were fighting weren't local—they were outsiders—black and white—who just came looking for trouble. If there hadn't been so much in the newspapers about the National Front coming, then perhaps these outsiders wouldn't have bothered to turn up.

1 How often does the Carnival take place?

2 Why do you think some people wanted it banned?

3 Who are the National Front, and what is their policy?

4 a) What do you think happened at the Carnival before the violence started?
  b) How exactly did the violence start?

5 What did the following groups do after that?
  a) the police
  b) the youths
  c) the National Front

6 What opinion does each of the four speakers have about what happened? ⟫→

Discussion

Who, in your opinion, was most to blame for the violence?

a) the Carnival organisers
b) the black community
c) the white community
d) the National Front
e) youths from outside the area
f) the police

Say what you think each group
should/shouldn't have done,
and why.

Writing

Write a letter to a newspaper expressing your views on who was to blame for the
violence. Take any point of view you like.

23.8 WHOSE FAULT?   Free practice

Work in groups.
Think of *either* a recent disaster (e.g. an air crash)
          or a social or economic problem (e.g. unemployment)
          or a recent violent incident (e.g. football hooliganism).

Discuss why it happened, whose fault it is, and how it could have been avoided.

Unit 23   Summary of language

In this unit you have learnt how to:
- say what's wrong with present situations
- criticise people's present behaviour
- criticise past actions and events
- speculate about imaginary situations
- blame people for what has happened

KEY POINTS

1 *Should/shouldn't*
   He **should** keep his café cleaner.
   You **shouldn't be** work**ing** so hard.
   She **should have** stay**ed** in bed.
   You **shouldn't have been** driv**ing** so fast.

2 *If + Past tense*
   If he clean**ed** his café, he **would** get more customers.
   If you **didn't** watch TV so much, you**'d** have more time for work.

3 *If + had(n't) done/had(n't) been doing*
   If she**'d** stay**ed** in bed, her temperature **would have** gone down.
   If you **hadn't** shouted at him, he **wouldn't have** walk**ed** out.
   If he**'d been** watching the toast, it **wouldn't have** burnt.
   If you **hadn't been** driv**ing** so fast, you **wouldn't have** skidd**ed**.

4 *Keeps doing/is always doing*
   He's a bore – he **keeps** talk**ing** about himself.
   Mary's so absent-minded – she**'s always** forget**ting** things.

Unit 24   Explanations

24.1   KINDS OF EXPLANATION

Presentation and practice

A

One of the reasons why so many children
start smoking is that they see adults
smoking: they think that it's a 'grown-up'
thing to do. They smoke in order to impress
their friends, and also because they don't
really believe that cigarettes will do them any
harm. Quite reasonably, they are not
impressed when adults warn them about the
dangers of smoking: if smoking is so
dangerous, why do so many adults do it?

B

Smoking can cause cancer, bronchitis and
heart disease. The nicotine inhaled from
cigarettes makes the heart beat faster, and
makes the arteries contract: this can lead to
blockages in the arteries, particularly in the
legs. Cancer and bronchitis are caused by the
tar and carbon monoxide taken into the
lungs. Although these harmful effects are
well known, people continue to smoke. Some
people carry on even after having a heart
attack or a leg amputated.

C

Action on Smoking and Health (ASH) exists
in order to make the public more aware of
the dangers of smoking. It tries to make
people give up the habit by organising anti-
smoking campaigns, and it is especially
concerned with limiting cigarette advertising.
So far, it has succeeded in persuading the
Government to ban cigarette advertising on
television.

1 In three sentences, say what each paragraph explains.
2 According to paragraph A, why do children start smoking?
3 According to paragraph B, what diseases can smoking cause? What is each disease
   caused by?
4 What is the purpose of ASH? What particular things does it do?

Practice

Work in groups. Discuss the following:

1 Do you agree with the reasons given in paragraph 1? What other reasons do you think there might be?
2 Why do you think people carry on smoking although they know the harmful effects of smoking?
3 What else can anti-smoking campaigns do to discourage people from smoking?

24.2 GIVING REASONS   Practice

Example Peter sold his car and bought a motorcycle . . .

  . . . **in order to** save money.
  . . . **so that** he could park in the city centre.
  . . . **because** he didn't want to get stuck in traffic jams.
  . . . **because** petrol had become so expensive.

Why do you think these people did what they did?

1 Angela sold her house in the country and bought a flat in London.
2 Frank decided to take up karate.
3 Joanna started learning English.
4 Colin decided to retire early, at 55.
5 Pauline stopped smoking.

Work in groups. What are the three most important decisions you ever made? Tell the others exactly what you did, and explain why.

24.3 GENERAL PURPOSE

Practice

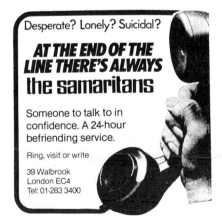

Desperate? Lonely? Suicidal?

AT THE END OF THE LINE THERE'S ALWAYS the samaritans

Someone to talk to in confidence. A 24-hour befriending service.

Ring, visit or write

39 Walbrook
London EC4
Tel: 01-283 3400

. . . a pleasant evening at home?

60,000 people in Britain have nowhere to go.

Help us to help them.

SHELTER
The National Campaign for the Homeless

When did you last taste **real** *cheese?*

Support the
Campaign for
Real Cheese
and bring the taste
back to cheese.

1 Suggest what each of these organisations is for. Use the expressions below:

  The purpose of .... **is to** ....
  .... **exists in order to** ....
  .... **is concerned with** .... -ing ....

2 What do you think each organisation does to achieve its aims?

Work in pairs.
Student A: You are a spokesman for one of the organisations above (or for another
organisation you know well). Answer student B's questions.
Student B: You are a journalist. Interview student A about the purpose of his/her
organisation, and what it does.

Writing

Write a paragraph about the organisation you discussed.

24.4 CAUSES AND RESULTS

Presentation

You will hear someone talking about conflict between teenagers and the law. Listen
to the tape and answer the questions.

1 a) According to the speaker, what is the main cause of teenagers coming into
conflict with the law?
  b) What exactly does he say?

2 What exactly does he say using:
  a) because of
  b) makes
  c) as a result
  d) lead to

3 What kind of 'trouble' do you think the speaker means?

Practice

Work in groups.
Which of the things below do you think are significant causes of conflict between teenagers and the law? Explain how they contribute to the problem.

parents   the police
school   TV and films
the urban environment

Writing

Choose two of the topics, and write two paragraphs based on your discussion.

24.5 EXPLANATIONS QUIZ   Free practice

1 What is the purpose of:
    a) Amnesty International?
    b) the AA?
    c) Oxfam?

2 What causes:
    a) earthquakes?
    b) tides?

3 How did the *Titanic* sink?

4 Why did:
    a) Thor Heyerdal sail from South America to Polynesia?
    b) President Nixon resign?

5 Why do:
    a) birds migrate?
    b) giraffes have long necks?

Now think of three 'explanations' questions of your own.

24.6 NOT WHAT YOU'D EXPECT   Presentation and practice

He looked very scruffy, but he still got the job.

A **Although**
   Even though | he looked very scruffy, he got the job.

B **In spite of**
   Despite | **the fact that** he looked scruffy, he got the job.

C **In spite of**
   Despite | his scruffy appearance, he got the job.

Change the sentences below in the same way, (a) with **although/even though** (b) with **in spite of/despite**.

1 She was 85 years old, but she still lived a very active life.
2 Video machines are expensive, but lots of people are buying them.
3 Her parents objected, but she still insisted on getting married.
4 Beethoven was deaf, but he continued composing until his death.
5 The acoustics in the hall are poor, but it is still regularly used for concerts.
6 We've known each other for a long time, but we still call each other by our surnames.
7 Hammerfest is a long way north of the Arctic Circle, but the sea never freezes there.

Work in groups of three. You are students A, B and C.
Read through your own section only, and then play the game, starting with student A.

Examples   A: Because of the cold weather . . .
              B or C: . . . we kept the fire on all day.
              A: In spite of the cold weather . . .
              B or C: . . . we all wore shorts.

Student A
Read out sentences 1–3 twice: (a) with
because of (b) with **in spite of**. B and C will
complete each sentence.

1 The weather was cold . . .
2 He was ill . . .
3 There's a meat shortage . . .

Choose one of these sentences to complete
what B and C read out.

. . . everyone thinks he's a tourist.
. . . the council demolished it.
. . . most people run a car.
. . . he was asked to appear on TV.
. . . they enjoyed living there.
. . . there were enough seats for everyone.
. . . we have no problem understanding him.
. . . there were a lot of accidents.
. . . there are fewer tourists here this year.
. . . he decided not to write any more.
. . . he drove at 60 m.p.h. all the way.
. . . we couldn't see what was going on.

Student B
Read out sentences 1–3 twice: (a) with
because of (b) with **in spite of**. A and C will
complete each sentence.

1 His book was successful . . .
2 There was ice on the roads . . .
3 The cost of living in Britain is high . . .

Choose one of these sentences to complete
what A and C read out.

. . . we kept the fire on all day.
. . . there were enough seats for everyone.
. . . everyone's living on beans.
. . . we have no problem understanding him.
. . . he managed to come to work.
. . . they enjoyed living there.
. . . we couldn't see what was going on.
. . . we all wore shorts.
. . . we've managed to get a leg of lamb.
. . . the council demolished it.
. . . everyone thinks he's a tourist.
. . . he had to cancel the appointment.

Student C
Read out sentences 1–3 twice: (a) with
because of (b) with **in spite of**. A and B will
complete each sentence.

1 There were large crowds . . .
2 He has a foreign accent . . .
3 The house was in bad condition . . .

Choose one of these sentences to complete
what A and B read out.

. . . there were a lot of accidents.
. . . he decided not to write any more.

. . . he was asked to appear on TV.
. . . we all wore shorts.
. . . he drove at 60 m.p.h. all the way.
. . . we've managed to get a leg of lamb.
. . . most people run a car.
. . . he had to cancel the appointment.
. . . everyone's living on beans.
. . . he managed to come to work.
. . . there are fewer tourists here this year.
. . . we kept the fire on all day.

24.8 OUT OF THE ORDINARY   Free practice

Work in groups. Tell the others about someone you know who lives in a way that
you find unusual or surprising. Say:
1 what is unusual about him/her
2 why you think he/she lives like that

24.9 SPOKES

Listening 📼

You will hear an interview with a woman who represents an organisation called
'Spokes'.

1 a) What is 'Spokes'?
  b) What are its two main purposes?

2 According to the woman, what
   facilities are provided for:
   a) pedestrians?
   b) motorists?
   c) cyclists?

3 a) What kind of cycle lanes does the
      woman think there should be?
  b) What kind of cycle lanes are there
      at the moment?

4 The woman gives two reasons why
   she thinks it is worth spending money
   on cycle lanes. What are they?

5 What exactly does she say about:
   a) the causes of accidents involving cyclists?
   b) why so few people in Britain cycle in cities?
   c) the effect of better facilities for cyclists?
   d) the attitude of British people to pollution
       and the energy crisis?
   e) the advantages of cycling?

6 a) The woman mentions three things that
      'Spokes' has done to promote its cause.
      What are they?
  b) In what two ways have they been successful?

Writing

Using information from the interview, write a paragraph of 100–150 words saying:
1 how facilities for cyclists in Britain are inadequate
2 what should be done about it

Discussion

Work in groups. Discuss:
1 what facilities are provided for cyclists in your country
2 what facilities you think should be provided

Unit 24 Summary of language

In this unit you have learnt how to:
– explain reasons
– explain purposes
– explain causes and results
– talk about unexpected results

KEY POINTS

1 *Reason and purpose*

Many people do yoga | **because** they want to keep fit.
| **in order to** keep fit.

She joined a drama group | **because** she felt lonely.
| **so that** she could meet people.

2 *General purpose*

The purpose of this organisation **is to** draw attention to the problems of
   old people.
Trade unions **exist in order to** protect workers.
'Actors Anonymous' **is** especially **concerned with** help**ing** young actors to
   establish themselves.

3 *Causes and results*

The hot weather **caused** many forest fires.
Many forest fires **were caused by** the hot weather.
As a result of cigarette price rises, many people are giving up smoking.
In the summer, thousands of tourists come to the town. **This** often

| **leads to** |
| **causes** | traffic congestion in the streets.

4 *'Concessive' structures*

Although/Even though he was very popular, he didn't win the election.

| **In spite of** |
| **Despite** | his popularity, he didn't win the election.

| **In spite of** |
| **Despite** | **the fact that** he was very popular, he didn't win the election.

5 *'Because' and 'because of'*

We stayed indoors | **because** there was fighting in the streets.
| **because of** the fighting in the streets.

| **Because of** the heavy rainfall, |
| **Because** it had rained so heavily, | many crops were destroyed.

178

Activities

CONTACT

You are going to a cocktail party. Your teacher will give you a role-card. When you get it:

1 Read it carefully, and put it in your pocket. *Do not show it to anyone else.*
2 Go to the cocktail party.

COMPOSITION

Write 150–200 words on *one* of the following:

1 Write a review for a newspaper of a recent film, play or book.
2 You recently bought *either* a car *or* a washing machine *or* a TV. You've had a lot of trouble with it ever since you bought it, and the after-sales service has been very unsatisfactory. Finally, you write a letter to the radio programme *Any Complaints?*, telling them about your problem.
3 Write a story about someone whose plans went horribly wrong.

JUST A MINUTE

Talk for *one* minute about one of the topics below, as fluently as you can. You can say anything you like about the topic, but try not to:

a) hesitate for too long   b) repeat yourself   c) make any mistakes

If you do, the teacher will stop you, and ask someone else to continue.

TOPICS

suntan oil	space travel	landladies	the street where	smoking
flying	hill-walking	hotels	you live	time
getting up	Africa	James Bond	saving money	
being a parent	Venice	flatmates	your future plans	
hiccups	parties	bathrooms	puppets	

ON THE ROCKS

Pair A: You are Ann, Bill's wife. You've been married for five years, and over the past couple of years your marriage hasn't been going very well. In your opinion, your husband:
1 has given too little attention to the children
2 has spent too much time at the pub with his friends, whom you dislike
3 hasn't helped you enough in the house
4 has only offered to take you out in the evening when he knows you're busy
5 has not given you enough money for housekeeping

You want to save your marriage, and decide to have a serious talk with him. Think of some of the things you will say, including how you will answer *his* criticisms of *you*.

Pair B: You are Bill, Ann's husband. You've been married for five years, and over the past couple of years your marriage hasn't been going very well. In your opinion, your wife:
1 has given all her attention to the children, not to you
2 hasn't tried to make herself look attractive
3 hasn't done enough housework or cooking
4 has been rude to several of your friends
5 has often unreasonably refused to go out with you

You want to save your marriage, and decide to have a serious talk with her. Think of some of the things you will say, including how you will answer *her* criticisms of *you*.

Now form new pairs (one A and one B) and have your discussion.

SITUATIONS

1 Someone you don't like invites you to a party tomorrow evening. Make an excuse.
2 You are with a friend who is trying on a coat in a shop. You don't think it looks good. Advise her not to buy it, and say why.
3 Someone asks you 'What's "Spokes"?' What do you say?
4 Your sister is upset because her boyfriend has left her. You think it's her own fault. Tell her so, and why.
5 A foreigner wants to study at a university in your country. Advise him what to do.
6 There was a road accident yesterday near your house. You arrived on the scene a few minutes after the accident. Describe what you saw.
7 You recently took up yoga. A friend asks you why. Explain.
8 Explain the rules of *Just a Minute*.

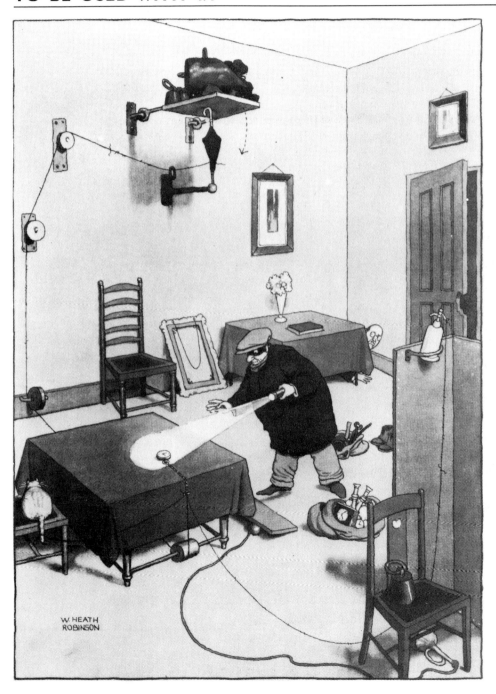

Listening texts

1.1 ROOMS AND FURNITURE 📼

Landlady: 447 4716.
Student: Hello. Is that Mrs Davies?
Landlady: Speaking.
Student: Good afternoon. My name's Stephen Brent. I was given your address by the student accommodation agency. I understand you have a room to let.
Landlady: Yes, that's right. I've just got one room still vacant. It's an attic room, on the second floor. It's rather small, but I'm sure you'll find it's very comfortable.
Student: I see. And how much do you charge for it?
Landlady: The rent's £25 a week. That includes electricity, but not gas.
Student: Has the room got central heating?
Landlady: No, it's got a gas fire which keeps the room very warm.
Student: I see ... And what about furniture? It is furnished, isn't it?
Landlady: Oh yes ... Er ... There's a divan bed in the corner with a new mattress on it. Er ... Let me see ... There's a small wardrobe, an armchair, a coffee table, a bookshelf ...
Student: Is there a desk?
Landlady: Yes, there's one under the window. It's got plenty of drawers and there's a lamp on it.
Student: Oh good ... Is there a washbasin in the room?
Landlady: No, I'm afraid there isn't a washbasin. But there's a bathroom just across the corridor, and that's got a washbasin and a shower as well as a bath. You share the bathroom with the people in the other rooms. The toilet is separate, but unfortunately it's on the floor below.
Student: Oh, that's all right ... What about cooking? Can I cook my own meals?
Landlady: Well, there's a little kitchenette next to your room. It hasn't got a proper cooker in it, but there's a gas ring and an electric kettle by the sink. I find my students prefer to eat at the university.
Student: I see. And is the room fairly quiet?
Landlady: Oh yes. It's at the back of the house. It looks onto the garden and it faces south, so it's bright and sunny, too. It's very attractive, really. And it's just under the roof, so it's got a low, sloping ceiling. Would you like to come and see it? I'll be in for the rest of the day.
Student: Yes, I'm very interested. It sounds like the kind of room I'm looking for. Can you tell me how to get there?
Landlady: Oh, it's very easy. The house is only five minutes' walk from Finchley Road tube station. Turn right outside the station, and then it's the third street on the left. You can't miss it. It's got the number on the gate. It's exactly opposite the cemetery.

1.7 TALKING ABOUT AMENITIES 📼

Visitor: Where can I stay in this town?
Resident: There are lots of hotels, but they tend to be fairly expensive. And then there are bed and breakfast places, which are much cheaper – and you can find out about

them through looking in the paper, or else just walking around the streets, and they have signs in the window saying 'Bed & Breakfast'. And then there are youth hostels.

Visitor: What are the youth hostels like?
Resident: The youth hostels are OK. All you get is a bed, but they do tend to be very cheap.
Visitor: Do I have to become a member?
Resident: Yes, you do, in fact. But it's very easy to join, and there's an office along the road, where you can go and sign on.

2.4 INTENTIONS AND PLANS 🖭

1st Student: Well, first of all I'm intending to have a good long holiday abroad, just travelling round Europe, and then when I get tired of travelling I'm going to – well, come back and start looking for a job. I haven't quite decided yet what job, but I'm probably going to try and get a job in advertising of some kind.
2nd Student: Well eventually I'm planning to open my own restaurant. Only I haven't got enough money to do that at the moment of course, so I've decided to get a temporary job for a year or so, and I'm going to work really hard and try and save as much money as possible. Actually, I'm thinking of working as a waiter, or some job in a restaurant anyway ...

5.1 RELATING PAST EVENTS 🖭

Interviewer: Now let's go back to your first novel, *Rag Doll*. When did you write that?
Writer: *Rag Doll*, yes. I wrote that in 1960, a year after I left school.
Interviewer: How old were you then?
Writer: Um, eighteen? Yes eighteen, because a year later I went to Indonesia.
Interviewer: Mm. And of course it was your experience in Indonesia that inspired your film *Eastern Moon*.
Writer: Yes that's right, although I didn't actually make *Eastern Moon* until 1978.
Interviewer: And you worked in television for a time too.
Writer: Yes, I started making documentaries for television in 1973, when I was 30. That was after I gave up farming.
Interviewer: Farming?
Writer: Yes, that's right. You see, I stayed in Indonesia for eight years. I met my wife there in 1965, and after we came back we bought a farm in the West of England, in 1970. A kind of experiment, really.
Interviewer: But you gave it up three years later.
Writer: Well yes you see it was very hard work, and I was also very busy working on my second novel, *The Cold Earth*, which came out in 1975.
Interviewer: Yes, that was a best-seller, wasn't it?
Writer: Yes it was, and that's why only two years after that I was able to give up television work and concentrate on films ...

7.6 REPORTING OFFERS 🖭

Henry: Cigarette?
Tony: Oh ... er ... thanks, Henry ... Um, do you have a light?
Henry: Sorry. Here.
Tony: Thanks. Lovely day. Pity I'm on duty.
Henry: I'll stand in for you if you like. I've got nothing else to do.
Tony: Oh no, I couldn't possibly ...
Henry: Go on. Go off and have a good time. Here – you can have the Mini if you like.

Tony: But . . . are you sure, Henry?
Henry: Of course I am. Take Jill up the mountains, or something.
Tony: That's ever so good of you, Henry. Oh, you . . . er . . . you won't tell anyone, will you . . . I mean, I am on duty.
Henry: Not a word. Bye, Tony – enjoy yourself.
Tony: Thanks Henry. I won't forget this . . .
Henry: Damned right you won't, you poor fool!

8.4   THE PRESENT PERFECT CONTINUOUS 🔲

Alan: Hello, Charles – I haven't seen you all day. What have you been doing?
Charles: Actually, I've been working on my first novel.
Alan: Oh yes? How far have you got with it?
Charles: Well, I've thought of a good title, and I've made a list of characters, and I've designed the front cover . . .
Alan: Have you started writing it yet?
Charles: Oh yes, I've written two pages already.
Alan: Only two?
Charles: Well yes – I haven't quite decided yet what happens next.

10.3   REMEMBERING THE PAST 🔲

I remember sailing on a pond that used to be by my grandfather's sawmill – we had a boat, and we used to go sailing on this. Also, we used to do a lot of climbing trees. We used to climb these trees for apples, which we then ate and made ourselves very sick. And my mother would come along and complain very strongly, but I don't think that stopped us at all. And of course in those days I had a bike, too, and I remember I used to push it up this very long hill near our house and then I'd get on and ride down as fast as I could go. My mother used to complain about that, too.

11.3   PREFERENCES 🔲

Woman: Which do you prefer: driving a car yourself or being a passenger?
Man: Well – that depends. I enjoy driving, especially on long empty roads where I can go nice and fast. But I'm not very fond of sitting in traffic jams waiting for lights to change, and things like that. I suppose I don't mind being a passenger, but only if I'm sure that the other person really can drive properly.
Woman: So you don't really like being in other people's cars, then?
Man: Well, as I say, it's all right with a good driver. Then I can relax, sit back and enjoy the scenery. But yes, you're right – on the whole I certainly prefer driving to being a passenger.

12.4   EXPERIENCES 🔲

A: Have you ever been chased by a dog, Keith?
B: No I haven't, but I have been chased by a bull.
A: Really?
B: Yes, it was a couple of weekends ago – I was, er, I was going for a walk out in the country following this footpath and it went through a field, and I was so busy looking out for the footpath that I didn't notice that the field was full of young bullocks. And the trouble was I was wearing this bright red anorak, and suddenly the bulls started bucking and jumping up and down and started chasing me.

C: What did you do?

B: Well I was pretty scared – I just ran for the nearest fence and jumped over it.

C: Actually I do know somebody who once got bitten by a dog while he was jogging.

A: Was he? How did that happen?

C: Well he was running past a farm when suddenly this sheepdog came out and started barking at him, so he tried to kick it out of the way but then suddenly the dog jumped up and bit him in the leg. I think he had to go to the doctor to make sure it wasn't infected.

13.3 HOW MUCH? 🔲

A: Do you ski at all?

B: No I don't.

A: Do you play tennis?

B: Yes, I do.

A: How much?

B: Oh I play tennis quite a lot.

A: What about gardening? Do you do any gardening?

B: Yes.

A: Do you do a lot of gardening?

B: No I don't do very much.

13.4 KINDS OF PEOPLE 🔲

He's quite a solitary type of person, really. You know, he spends most of his time at home, reading, listening to the radio, things like that. He goes out to the pub occasionally, and he does quite a lot of singing, too – he belongs to the local choir, I believe – but you never see him at weekends. He's always off somewhere in the country, walking or fishing. He does a lot of fishing, actually – but always on his own. Funny sort of bloke.

14.3 PROBLEMS 🔲

My problem is with my mother, who is now well over 70 and a widow and becoming very fragile, and she really needs my help. But where she lives, in the country, there's no work available for me – I'm a designer – and she can't come and live with me because she says she doesn't like the climate because it's too bad for her rheumatism, which is actually true – it's very cold here. And if I go and work there as something else where she lives, perhaps as a secretary, it means we have to take a drastic drop in salary. So I don't really know what to do.

15.1 ORIGIN AND DURATION 🔲

Dialogue 1

A: Hmm. You're a good squash player. How long have you been playing?

B: Oh, I've been playing since the beginning of last term. What about you?

A: Me? Oh, I've been playing for about two years now – but I'm still not very good.

Dialogue 2

A: I suppose you know how to waltz, do you?

B: Yes, but not very well, I'm afraid. I only learnt a few weeks ago. When did you learn?

A: Oh, I learnt to waltz in about 1970 – just after I left school. Er – shall we dance, then?

Dialogue 3

A: And this is my cousin, Sue.
B: Ah yes – we already know each other actually.
A: Do you? How long have you known each other, then?
B: Oh, we've known each other for about six months now, I think, haven't we?
C: Oh no much longer than that. We met about a year ago, at that Christmas party – remember?

17.6 TASTES IN COMMON

Woman A: I can't stand places like Majorca or the Costa Brava.
Man: No, nor can I.
Woman A: You know, where you have to share the beach with thousands of other people and everyone speaks English.
Woman B: Oh I don't mind that.
Man: Oh I do. I never go to places like that. I like to get right away from all the tourists, go somewhere that's really quiet and peaceful, like an island or something.
Woman A: Yes, so do I – where no-one speaks English.
Woman B: What's wrong with people speaking English? I like meeting people when I'm on holiday. I like places with a good night life, and plenty of men around, and . . . well, you know, where you can have a good time . . .

18.6 FREEDOM OF CHOICE

When parents make a lot of rules about their children's behaviour, they make trouble – for themselves. I used to spend half my time making sure my rules were obeyed, and the other half answering questions like 'Jack can get up whenever he likes, so why can't I?' or 'Why can't I play with Angela? Jack's mum doesn't mind who *he* plays with.' or 'Jack can drink anything he likes. Why can't I drink wine too?' Jack's mum, I decided, was a wise woman. I started saying things like 'Of course, dear. You can drink as much wine as you like.' and 'No, I don't mind how late you get up.' and 'Yes, dear, you can play with Angela as often as you like.' The results have been marvellous. They don't want to get up late any more, they've decided they don't like wine, and, most important, they've stopped playing with Angela. I've now realised (as Jack's mum realised a long time ago) that they only wanted to do all these nasty things because they weren't allowed to.

19.1 DEGREES OF PROBABILITY

A: No luck then, John?
B: Afraid not, sir. Not yet, anyhow. We're still checking on stolen cars.
A: Mm.
B: Where do you think he'll head for, sir?
A: Well, he definitely won't try to leave the country yet. He may try to get a passport, and he'll certainly need clothes and money. He'll probably get in touch with Cornfield for those, so I expect he'll make for Birmingham.
B: Right. I'll put some men on the house.
A: Yes, do that. Mind you, I doubt if he'll show up there in person. Hammond's no fool, you know. I should think he'll probably telephone.
B: What about his wife?
A: Mm. I shouldn't think he'll go anywhere near her – though he might get her to join him after he's left the country. And when he does leave, he probably won't use a major

airport, either. So you'd better alert the coastguard, and keep an eye on the private airfields.

B: Right, sir. I'd better get his description circulated.

A: Yes. He may change his appearance, of course, but I don't expect he'll be able to do much about the tattoos . . . And John – be careful. He could be armed. And if I know Hammond, he certainly won't give himself up without a fight.

20.2 THE LOST PROPERTY OFFICE

Assistant: Good morning, sir.

Man: Good morning. I wonder if you can help. I've lost my coat.

Assistant: Where did you lose it, sir?

Man: Er . . . I left it on the . . . um . . . underground yesterday morning.

Assistant: Can you describe it?

Man: Well, it's a full-length brown overcoat with a check pattern on it. It's got a wide belt, and one of those thick furry collars that keep your ears warm. It's a very nice coat, actually.

Assistant: Hmm. I'm afraid we haven't got anything like that, sir. Sorry.

Man: Well, to tell you the truth, I lost another coat last week. On the bus. It's a three-quarter length coat – it's grey, with big black buttons and a black belt.

Assistant: Sorry, sir. Nothing like that.

Man: Hmm. And then only this morning I left my white raincoat in a park. It's got a silk lining . . .

Assistant: Look, sir. I'm a busy woman. If you really need a coat so badly, there's a very good second-hand clothes shop just round the corner . . .

ACTIVITIES (following Unit 20): CALL MY BLUFF

Voice 1: Well, hunk is a verb. And it means to carry something, particularly something that's heavy and difficult to move. So you can say something like 'When I saw the men they were hunking the piano down the stairs'.

Voice 2: Actually, hunk is the cry made by an elephant, especially when it's angry, or it's trying to contact other elephants. The word sounds like the noise they make – 'hunk, hunk'. So you can say, for example, 'The elephants are hunking a lot tonight'.

Voice 3: No, no, the truth is, hunk is a noun. And it means a piece of something, a big thick piece. So if you cut a thin piece of bread, that's not a hunk. When you tear off a thick piece of bread, that's a hunk. Today, for example, I had a big hunk of bread and cheese for my lunch.

21.5 FAULTS AND REMEDIES

Woman: The trouble with education in Britain, I think, lies with the teachers. I don't think teachers get nearly enough training in actually how to teach rather than the subject. I think they're too serious, too academic, they're not imaginative enough. And that means that there's not enough excitement in the classroom for children to get interested in the subject.

Man: Yes, I agree. I think there's too much theoretical teaching given and not enough practical education, with the result that pupils are far too busy studying for exams to have time to learn about life itself and how to, how to live in the world.

Woman: Mm. I think all teachers should be at least 25 before they start teaching. I think they should be forced to live in the outside world, rather than go from the classroom to the university and back to the classroom again.

22.1 SETTING A SCENE

Extract 1

It was early afternoon, and the beach was almost empty. It was getting hot now. Most of the tourists were still finishing their lunch back at the hotel, or taking their afternoon siesta in the air-conditioned comfort of their rooms. One or two Englishmen were still lying stretched out on the sand, determined to go home with a good suntan, and a few local children were splashing around in the clear shallow water. There was a large yacht moving slowly across the bay. The girl was on board. She was standing at the back of the boat, getting ready to dive. Jason put on his sunglasses and casually wandered down towards the sandy beach . . .

Extract 2

Jacqueline got out of the bus and looked around her. It was typical of the small villages of that part of the country. The houses stood in two long lines on either side of the dusty road which led to the capital. In the square, the paint was peeling off the Town Hall, and some small children were running up and down its steps, laughing. On the other side, there were a few old men sitting outside a café playing backgammon and smoking their pipes. A lonely donkey was quietly munching the long dry grass at the foot of the statue that stood in the centre of the square. Jacqueline sighed . . .

22.7 MEMORIES

Well, we met at a party in London. You see I'd just moved to London because of my job and I didn't really know anybody, and one of the people at work had invited me to this party and so there I was. But it was one of those boring parties, you know everybody was just sitting in small groups talking to people they knew already, and I was feeling really bored with the whole thing. And then I noticed this rather attractive girl sitting at the edge of one of the groups, and she was looking bored too, just about as bored as I was. And so we started, um, we started looking at each other, and then I went across and we started talking. And as it turned out she'd only just arrived in London herself so we had quite a bit in common – and well that's how it all started really.

ACTIVITIES (following Unit 22): ESKIMOS

A: Well it's got two big wheels one behind the other, and there's a kind of metal frame between the wheels that holds them together. And there's a little seat above the back wheel that you can sit on, and above the front wheel there's a sort of metal bar that sticks out on both sides. And you sit on the seat you see, and you put your hands on this metal bar thing – and the whole thing moves forwards – it's amazing.

B: What makes it move forward, then?

A: Ah well in the middle you see, between the two wheels, there are these other bits of metal and you can put your feet on these and turn them round and that makes the wheels go round.

B: Hang on – if it's only got two wheels why doesn't the whole thing fall over?

A: Well you see, um, well I'm not sure actually . . .

23.5 PAST MISTAKES

A: Me, officer? You're joking!
B: Come off it, Mulligan. For a start, you spent three days watching the house. You shouldn't have done that, you know. The neighbours got suspicious and phoned the police . . .
A: But I was only looking, officer.
B: . . . and on the day of the robbery, you really shouldn't have used your own car. We got your number. And if you'd worn a mask, you wouldn't have been recognised.
A: I didn't go inside!
B: Ah, there's another thing. You should've worn gloves, Mulligan. If you had, you wouldn't have left your fingerprints all over the house. We found your fingerprints on the jewels, too.
A: You mean . . . you've found the jewels?
B: Oh yes. Where you . . . er . . . 'hid' them. Under your mattress.
A: My God! You know everything! I'll tell you something, officer – you shouldn't have joined the police force. If you'd taken up burglary, you'd have made a fortune!

24.4 CAUSES AND RESULTS

Well, I think that this problem of teenagers getting into trouble with the law is mainly caused by unemployment. You see, because of the high level of unemployment, so many teenagers nowadays leave school and find that they have no chance of getting a job, and this obviously makes them feel bored and frustrated. And as a result of this, they're much more likely to get drunk and so on. Another thing of course is that you get groups of unemployed teenagers wandering around the streets with nothing to do, which can easily lead to trouble of one sort or another . . .

Drills

Drill 1   Having things done

Are you going to alter that suit yourself?
No I'm going to have it altered at the tailor's.

You're not going to develop those films yourself, are you?
No, I'm going to have them developed at the photographer's.

Drill 2   Spontaneous decisions

Apparently that new play is fantastic. (go and see)
Mm. In that case, I think I'll go and see it.

That cake looks horrible. (have)
Mm. In that case I don't think I'll have any.

Drill 3   Asking about intentions and plans

They're going to paint their kitchen either white or yellow.
What colour are they going to paint their kitchen?

He's thinking of going abroad either in March or in April.
When's he thinking of going abroad?

LAB SESSION 2 (UNITS 3–4)

Drill 1   Occupations

He drives buses.
Oh, so he's a bus driver, is he?

I deliver letters.
Oh, so you're a postman, are you?

Drill 2   Questions of routine

You want to know what time he gets up.
What time do you get up?

You want to know if his wife goes with him on tour.
Does your wife go with you on tour?

Drill 3   Things that happen

Do people ever criticise you in the newspapers? (occasionally).
Oh yes. I occasionally get criticised in the newspapers.

Does someone drive you to the studio? (always)
Oh yes. I always get driven to the studio.

LAB SESSION 3 (UNITS 5–6)

Drill 1   Events in sequence

Kate left university. Six months later she moved to London.
Six months after leaving university, Kate moved to London.

A few weeks after that she started work at IBM.
A few weeks after moving to London, she started work at IBM.

Drill 2   There is and there are

Three women are standing at the bus stop.
There are three women standing at the bus stop.

Nobody's using the car today.
There isn't anybody using the car today.

Drill 3   The Present Continuous Passive

So they're smuggling guns into the country, are they?
Yes, sir. Guns are being smuggled into the country.

And they're bringing them in in small boats, eh?
Yes, sir. They're being brought in in small boats.

LAB SESSION 4 (UNITS 7–8)

Drill 1   Would you mind?

Don't tell anyone.
Would you mind not telling anyone?

Can I take a key?
Would you mind if I took a key?

Drill 2   Reporting offers

Here. Have an apple.
He offered me an apple.

Would you like to lie down?
He offered to let me lie down.

It's all right. I'll pay for the meal.
He offered to pay for the meal.

Drill 3   Is everything ready?

When are the cleaners going to clean the theatre?
Don't worry. They've already cleaned it.

I hope we sell all the tickets.
It's all right. We've already sold them.

Drill 4   Recent activities

Darling, you know you told Billy not to fish in the river . . .
What? He's been fishing in the river again, has he?

And you asked Mrs Roberts to stop using your parking space . . .
What? She's been using my parking space again, has she?

LAB SESSION 5 (UNITS 9–10)

Drill 1   Comparison

I always think that cats aren't as clean as dogs.
Nonsense. Cats are much cleaner than dogs.

Students don't work as hard as teachers.
Nonsense. Students work much harder than teachers.

Drill 2   The past and the present

People used to die of smallpox.
People don't die of smallpox any longer.

Cranmore Castle is a language school now.
Cranmore Castle didn't use to be a language school.

Drill 3   Changes

Do they still live in Edinburgh? (move)
No, they've moved now.

Is that old hotel still there? (pull down)
No, it's been pulled down now.

Drill 4   Time comparison

Do you eat much?
Oh no, not as much as I used to.
Really?
Yes, I used to eat much more than I do now.

LAB SESSION 6 (UNITS 11–12)

Drill 1   Likes and dislikes

Shall we play cards? (love)
She loves playing cards.

Don't touch me! (loathe)
She loathes being touched.

Drill 2   Events and circumstances

Why does the sun always go in when I'm sunbathing?
Martin was sunbathing when the sun went in.

How is it that whenever I'm watching television there's an electricity cut?
Martin was watching television when there was an electricity cut.

Drill 3   Hearing things

(Sound of dogs barking)
I could hear some dogs barking.

(Man's voice: 'Be quiet')
I heard a man say 'Be quiet'.

LAB SESSION 7 (UNITS 13–14)

Drill 1   Skill

I'm fantastic at skiing, you know.
Yes, I know. You're a fantastic skier.

You're a useless dancer, you know.
Yes, I know. I'm useless at dancing.

Drill 2   Giving advice

Don't eat so much. (if)
If I were you, I wouldn't eat so much.

Join a slimming club. (try)
Have you tried joining a slimming club?

Drill 3   Giving advice with a reason

Take an umbrella – then you won't get wet. (so that)
You'd better take an umbrella so that you don't get wet.

Wear a raincoat – it might rain. (in case)
You'd better wear a raincoat in case it rains.

LAB SESSION 8 (UNITS 15–16)

Drill 1   Up to now

I arrived two days ago.
So you've been here for two days, have you?

Mary moved to London in April.
So she's been living in London since April, has she?

Drill 2   Ever since

Soon after she met Pierre, she had her first French lesson.
She's been having French lessons ever since she met Pierre.

Soon after he got his new hi-fi he got his first complaint from the neighbours.
He's been getting complaints from the neighbours ever since he got his new hi-fi.

Drill 3   Location

The house has got a study. (front)
There's a study at the front of the house.

The car's got a bullet hole. (side)
There's a bullet hole in the side of the car.

LAB SESSION 9 (UNITS 17–18)

Drill 1   Discovering similarities

I've had my car serviced.
So have I.

I don't like doing night-duty.
Nor do I.

I should go.
So should I.

Drill 2   Have to and allowed to

They made us wear a uniform.
What? You mean you had to wear a uniform?

They let us copy in exams, though.
What? You mean you were allowed to copy in exams?

Drill 3   Freedom of choice

Who can I bring to the party?
You can bring whoever you like.
Really?
Yes, I don't mind who you bring.

How late can I stay up?
You can stay up as late as you like.
Really?
Yes, I don't mind how late you stay up.

LAB SESSION 10 (UNITS 19–20)

Drill 1   Probabilities

'Will the stewardess give me some magazines?'
'She might, if you ask nicely.'
If you ask nicely the stewardess might give you some magazines.

'Will I be sick?'
'Probably not, unless the weather's bad.'
Unless the weather's bad, you probably won't be sick.

Drill 2   Will be doing and will have done

I do want to recover.
Don't worry. You'll have recovered by next week.

I want to play tennis again.
Don't worry. You'll be playing tennis again next week.

Drill 3   Describing objects: relative clauses

I need a pair of boots. I want to wear them for hillwalking.
I need a pair of boots that I can wear for hillwalking.

I'd love one of those cookers – you know, they light themselves.
I'd love one of those cookers that light themselves.

LAB SESSION 11 (UNITS 21–2)

Drill 1   Too and enough

You can sleep on this bed. It's a bit hard, I'm afraid.
Oh no. It's much too hard for me to sleep on.

Here, eat this – it's not very hot, I'm afraid.
Oh no. It's not nearly hot enough for me to eat.

Drill 2   So and such

My bed's terribly hard – I sometimes lie awake all night.
Her bed's so hard that she sometimes lies awake all night.

They serve really bad food – I can hardly eat it.
They serve such bad food that she can hardly eat it.

Drill 3   Past states and previous actions

His suitcase was packed.　　　　　*The lights were all switched off.*
He had packed his suitcase.　　　　He had switched off all the lights.

LAB SESSION 12 (UNITS 23–4)

Drill 1   Should and shouldn't

The children are playing in the road.
Well they shouldn't be playing in the road.

Paul didn't do his homework yesterday.
Well he should have done his homework.

Drill 2   Conditional sentences

'*I feel ill.*'
'*That's because you don't eat properly.*'
If you ate properly, you wouldn't feel ill.

'*I've lost my address book.*'
'*That's because you didn't put it away.*'
If you'd put it away, you wouldn't have lost it.

Drill 3   In spite of

It was dark but I could see them.
I could see them in spite of the darkness.

He's strong, but he couldn't break the door down.
He couldn't break the door down, in spite of his strength.